Originally launched on Facebook, Rupert Fawcett's brilliantly observed, touchingly truthful *Off The Leash* cartoons have developed a huge daily following around the world.

This book brings together the very best of those cartoons, featuring the secret thoughts and conversations of dogs of every size, shape, and breed. It is a celebration of our favorite belly-scratching, tail-chasing, bed-stealing canine friends—for dog lovers everywhere.

Off The Leash

THE SECRET LIFE OF DOGS

Rupert Fawcett

St. Martin's Griffin
New York

Printed in the United States of America. For information, address St. Martin's Press, 175 Fifth Avenue, New York, N.Y. 10010.

www.stmartins.com

Library of Congress Cataloging-in-Publication Data

Fawcett, Rupert.
[Off the leash. Selections]
Off the leash : the secret life of dogs / Rupert Fawcett. — First U.S. Edition.
p. cm.
ISBN 978-1-250-05956-7 (paper over board)
ISBN 978-1-4668-6471-9 (e-book)
1. Dogs—Caricatures and cartoons. 2. English wit and humor, Pictorial. I. Title.
NC1479.F39A4 2014
741.5'6941—dc23

2014027597

St. Martin's Griffin books may be purchased for educational, business, or promotional use. For information on bulk purchases, please contact Macmillan Corporate and Premium Sales Department at 1-800-221-7945, extension 5442, or write specialmarkets@macmillan.com.

First published in Great Britain by Boxtree, an imprint of Pan Macmillan, a division of Macmillan Publishers Limited

First U.S. Edition: October 2014

10 9 8 7 6 5 4 3 2 1

Foreword

I was brought up with dogs and have always found them comical as well as very lovable. About a year ago, I started drawing cartoons featuring talking dogs and was encouraged by friends to put them on a social media site. I then created an *Off The Leash* Facebook page and started posting one a day. I was amazed by the response and now have many thousands of people following the cartoons every day, all over the world. The cartoons appeal to all sorts of people, from passionate dog lovers who have eight sleeping on their bed at night, to people who don't have any pets at all, but can still identify with the characteristics. Let's face it, who doesn't like to be fed, have their tummy stroked and snooze on the sofa in the afternoon? This is my first *Off The Leash* compilation — I hope you enjoy it!

Rupert Fawcett

For Mandy

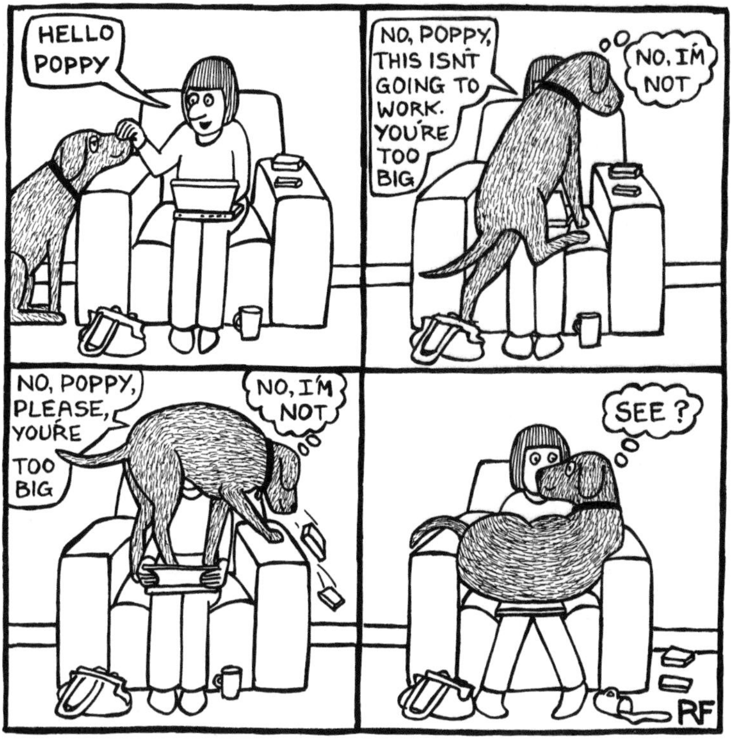
HELLO POPPY
NO, POPPY, THIS ISN'T GOING TO WORK. YOU'RE TOO BIG
NO, I'M NOT
NO, POPPY, PLEASE, YOU'RE TOO BIG
NO, I'M NOT
SEE?
RF

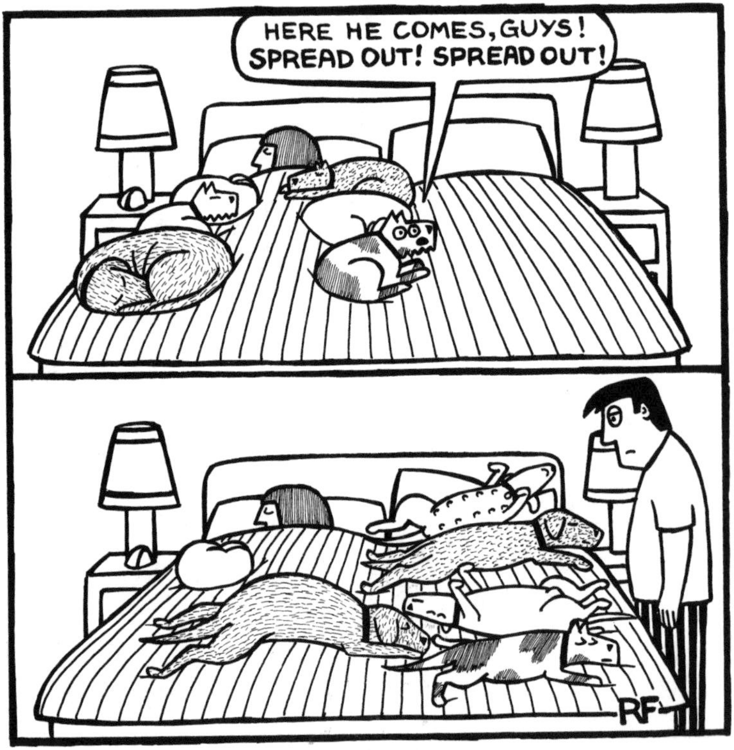
HERE HE COMES, GUYS! SPREAD OUT! SPREAD OUT!
RF

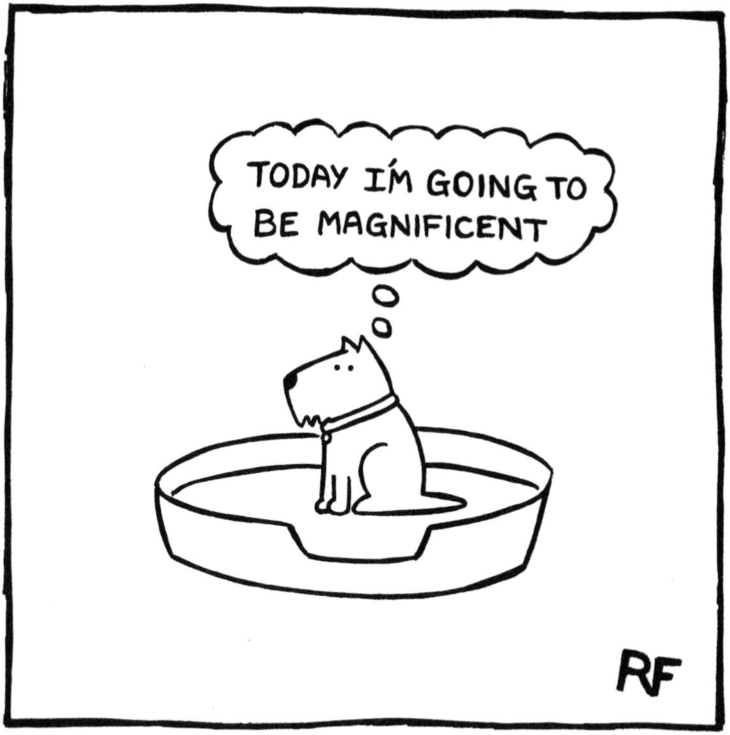
TODAY I'M GOING TO BE MAGNIFICENT
RF

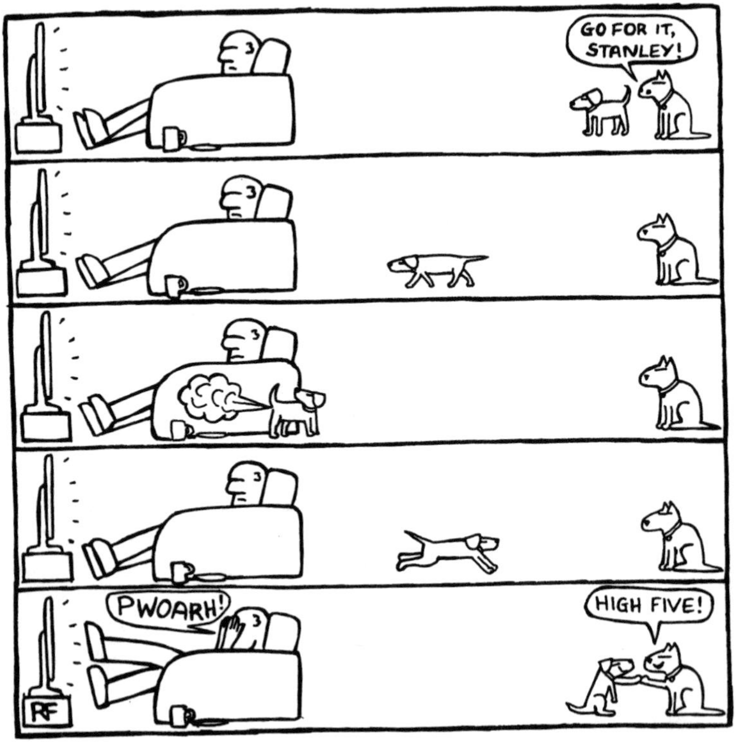
GO FOR IT, STANLEY!
PWOARH!
HIGH FIVE!
RF

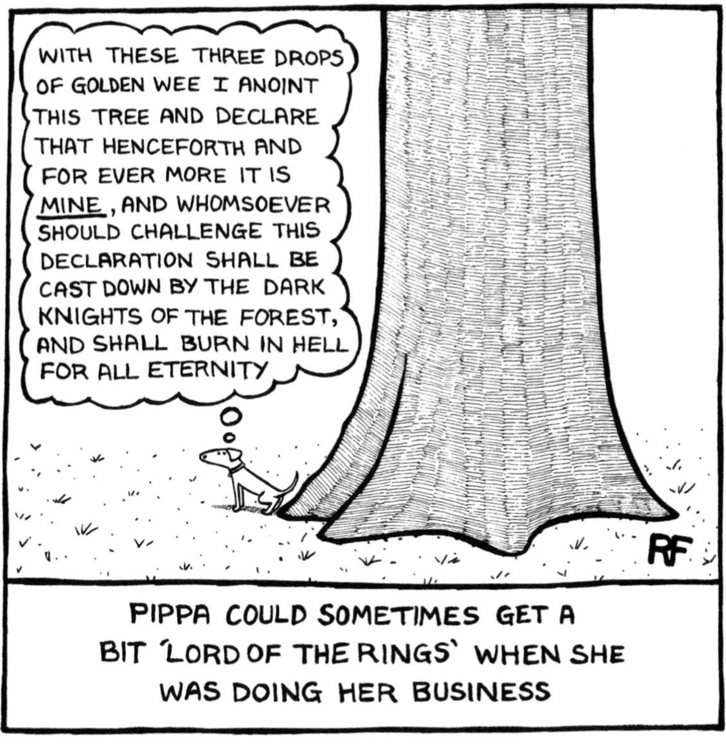
WITH THESE THREE DROPS OF GOLDEN WEE I ANOINT THIS TREE AND DECLARE THAT HENCEFORTH AND FOR EVER MORE IT IS MINE, AND WHOMSOEVER SHOULD CHALLENGE THIS DECLARATION SHALL BE CAST DOWN BY THE DARK KNIGHTS OF THE FOREST, AND SHALL BURN IN HELL FOR ALL ETERNITY
RF

PIPPA COULD SOMETIMES GET A BIT 'LORD OF THE RINGS' WHEN SHE WAS DOING HER BUSINESS

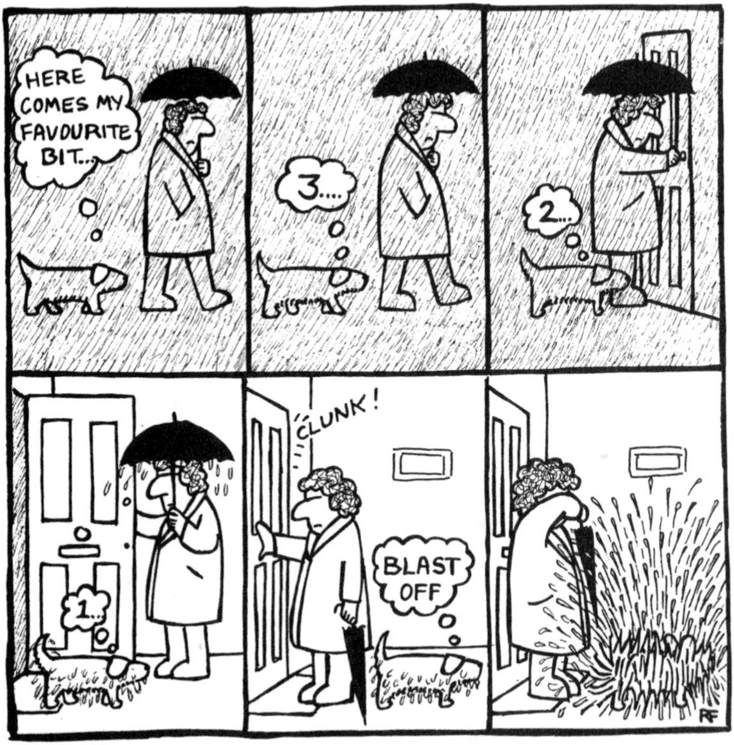
HERE COMES MY FAVOURITE BIT...
3....
2...
1...
CLUNK!
BLAST OFF
RF

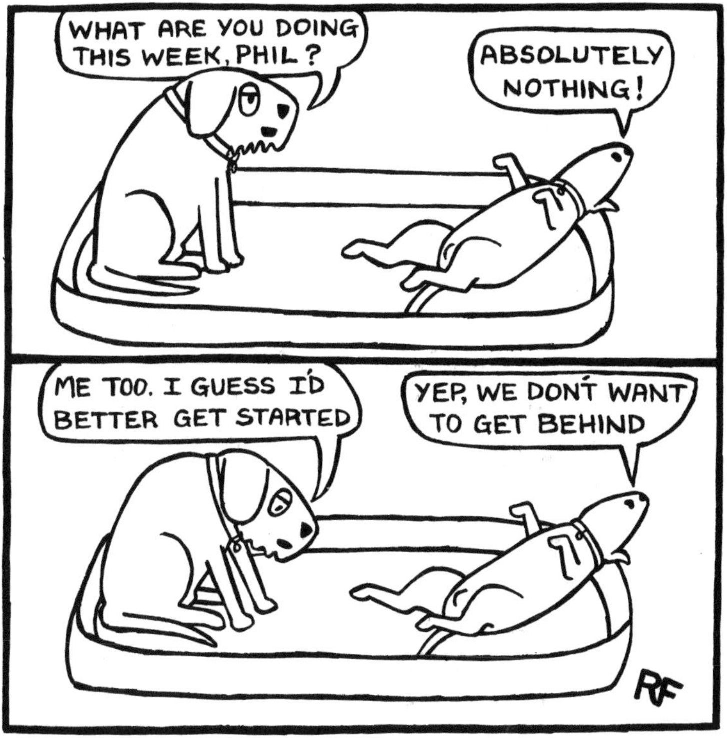
WHAT ARE YOU DOING THIS WEEK, PHIL?
ABSOLUTELY NOTHING!
ME TOO. I GUESS I'D BETTER GET STARTED
YEP, WE DON'T WANT TO GET BEHIND
RF

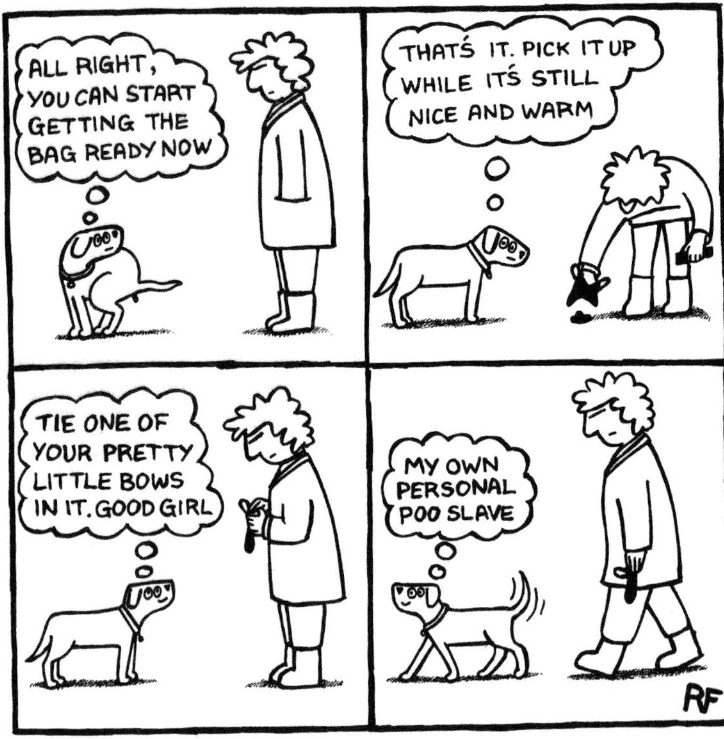
ALL RIGHT, YOU CAN START GETTING THE BAG READY NOW
THAT'S IT. PICK IT UP WHILE IT'S STILL NICE AND WARM
TIE ONE OF YOUR PRETTY LITTLE BOWS IN IT. GOOD GIRL
MY OWN PERSONAL POO SLAVE
RF

AT PUPPY SCHOOL...
TODAY'S LESSON
CHAOS AND DESTRUCTION
SO, MR LEIBOWITZ, WHAT YOU'RE SAYING IS THAT WHATEVER OUR OWNERS TELL US TO DO, WE SHOULD DO THE OPPOSITE, AND WE'LL NEVER GET IN SERIOUS TROUBLE BECAUSE WE ARE SO DAMN CUTE
PRECISELY
RF

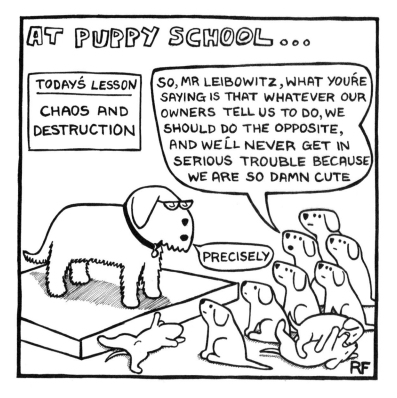

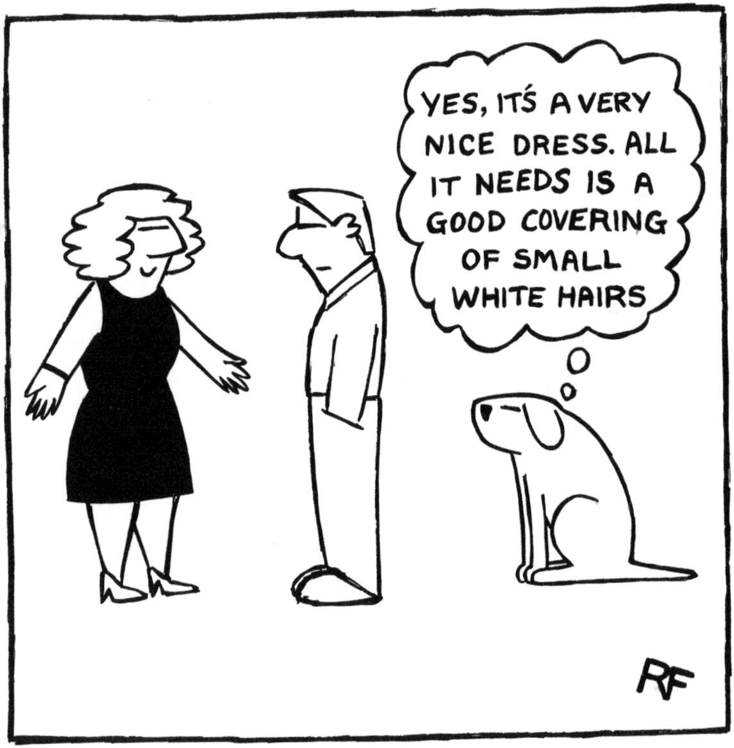
YES, IT'S A VERY NICE DRESS. ALL IT NEEDS IS A GOOD COVERING OF SMALL WHITE HAIRS
RF

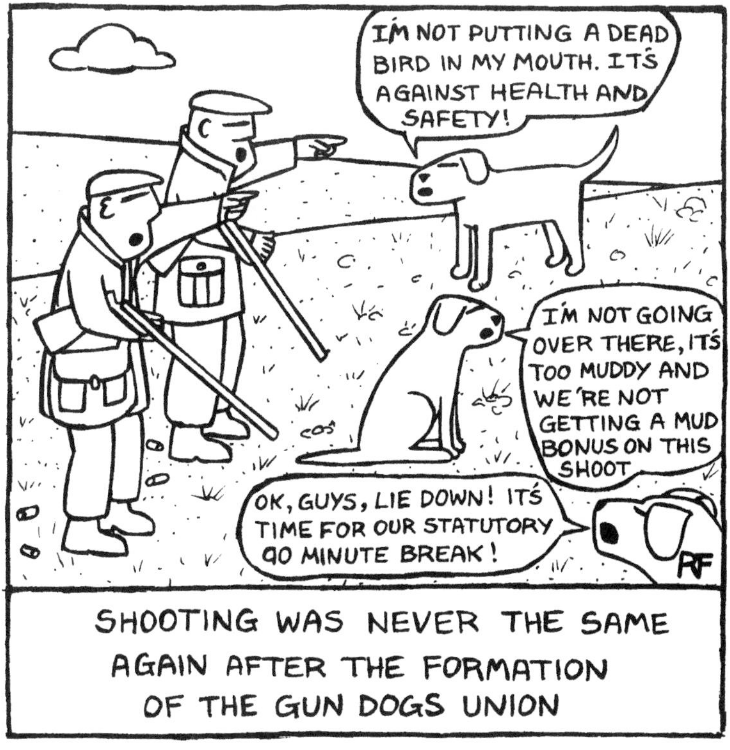
I'M NOT PUTTING A DEAD BIRD IN MY MOUTH. IT'S AGAINST HEALTH AND SAFETY!
I'M NOT GOING OVER THERE, IT'S TOO MUDDY AND WE'RE NOT GETTING A MUD BONUS ON THIS SHOOT
OK, GUYS, LIE DOWN! IT'S TIME FOR OUR STATUTORY 90 MINUTE BREAK!
RF

SHOOTING WAS NEVER THE SAME AGAIN AFTER THE FORMATION OF THE GUN DOGS UNION

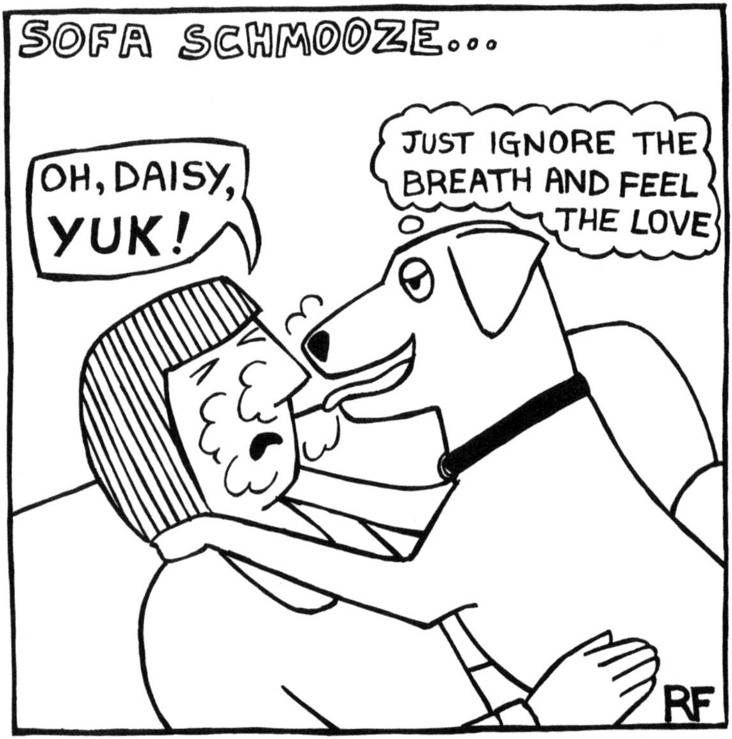
SOFA SCHMOOZE...
OH, DAISY, YUK!
JUST IGNORE THE BREATH AND FEEL THE LOVE
RF

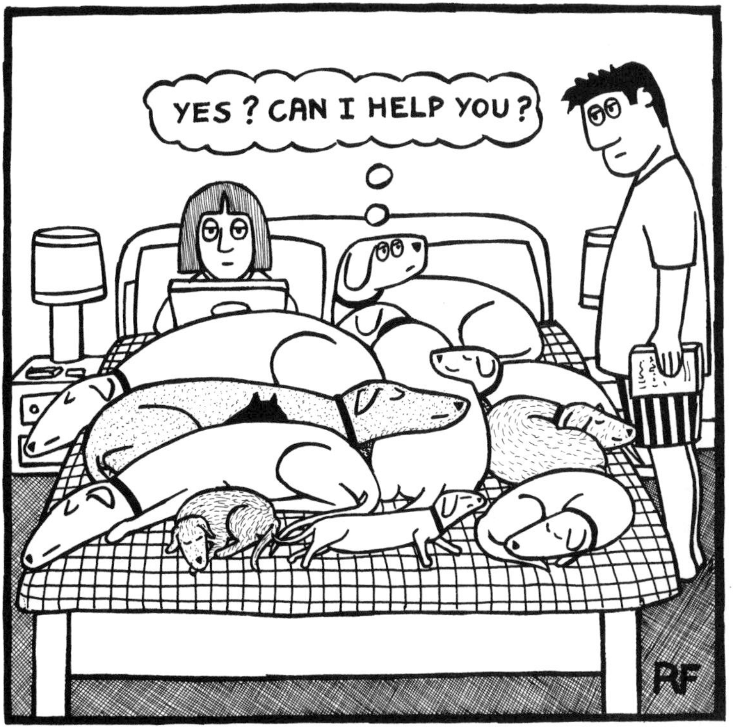
YES? CAN I HELP YOU?
RF

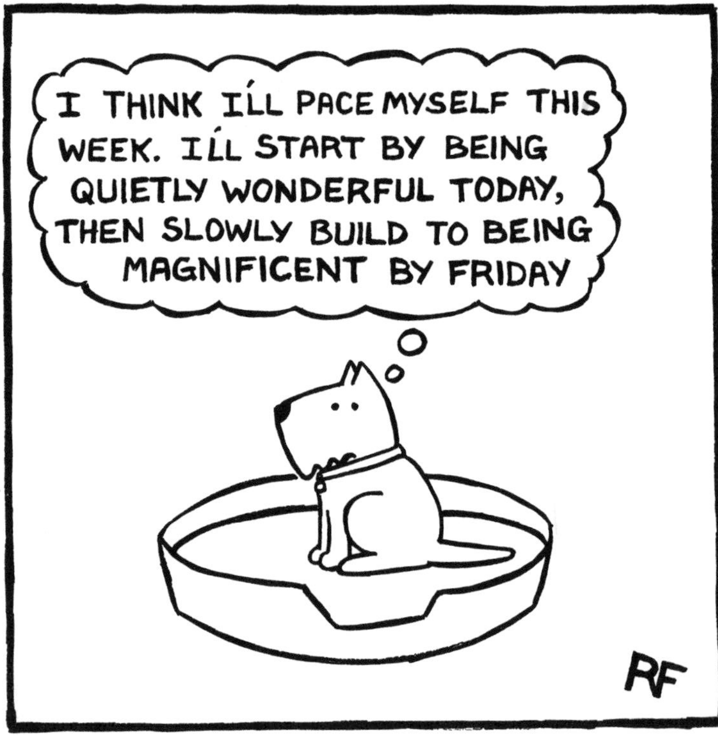
I THINK I'LL PACE MYSELF THIS WEEK. I'LL START BY BEING QUIETLY WONDERFUL TODAY, THEN SLOWLY BUILD TO BEING MAGNIFICENT BY FRIDAY
RF

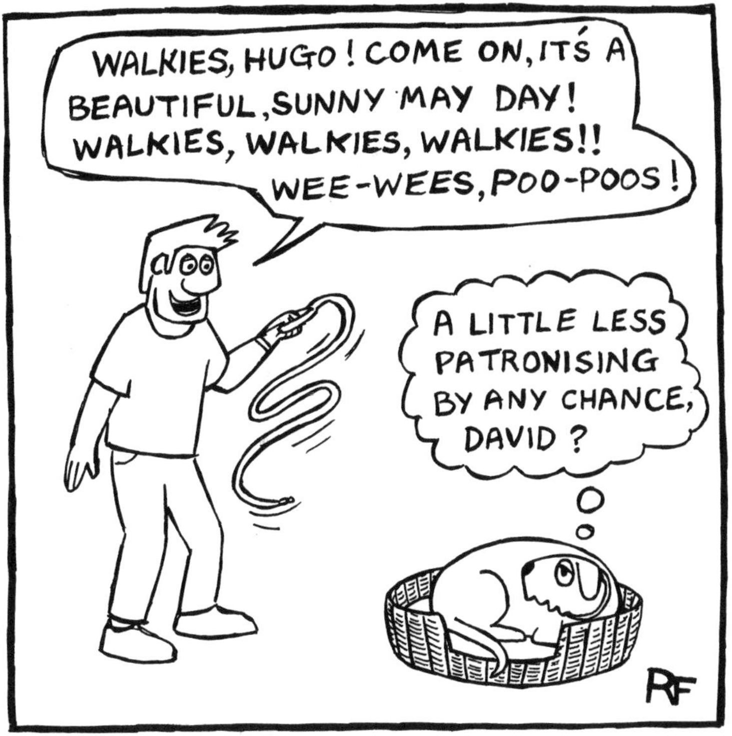
WALKIES, HUGO! COME ON, IT'S A BEAUTIFUL, SUNNY MAY DAY! WALKIES, WALKIES, WALKIES!! WEE-WEES, POO-POOS!
A LITTLE LESS PATRONISING BY ANY CHANCE, DAVID?
RF

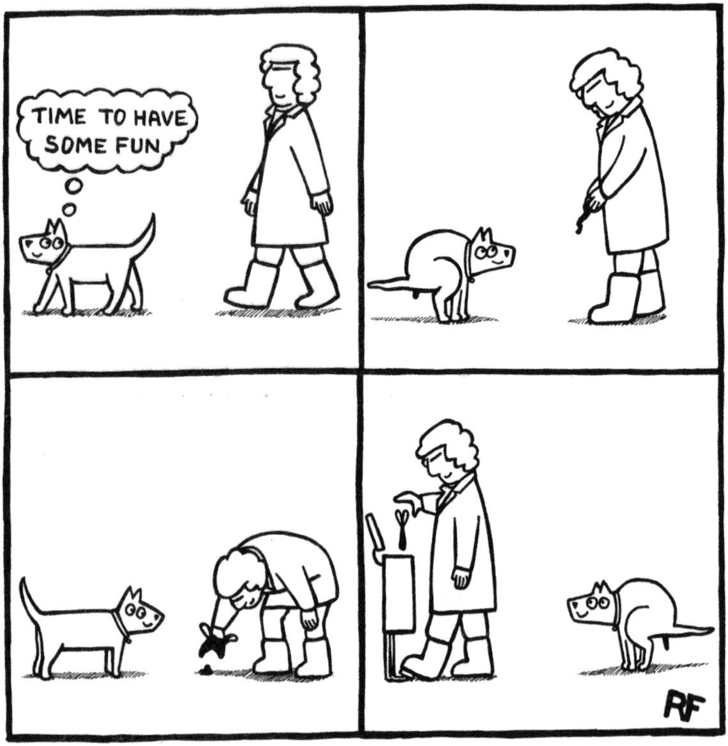
TIME TO HAVE SOME FUN
RF

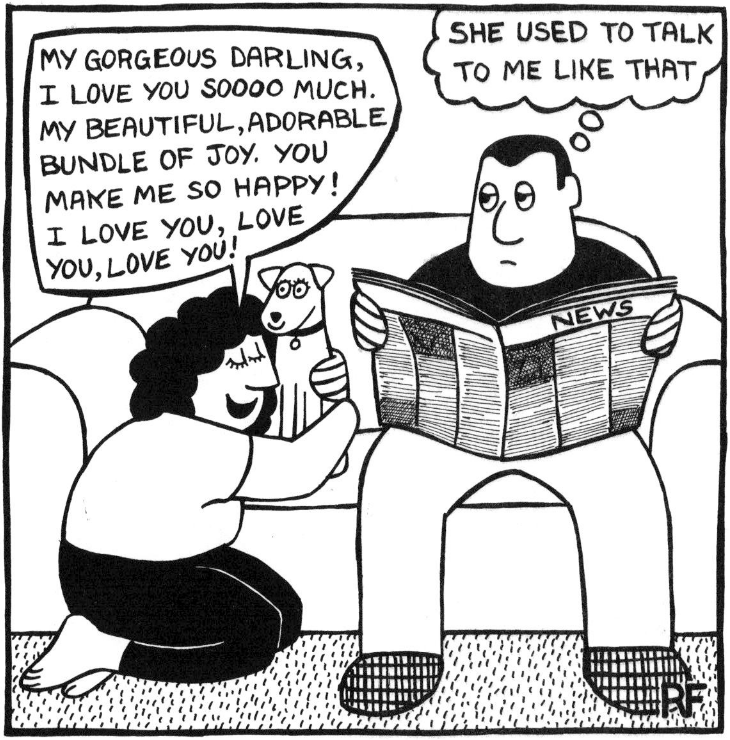
MY GORGEOUS DARLING, I LOVE YOU SOOOO MUCH. MY BEAUTIFUL, ADORABLE BUNDLE OF JOY. YOU MAKE ME SO HAPPY! I LOVE YOU, LOVE YOU, LOVE YOU!
SHE USED TO TALK TO ME LIKE THAT
NEWS
RF

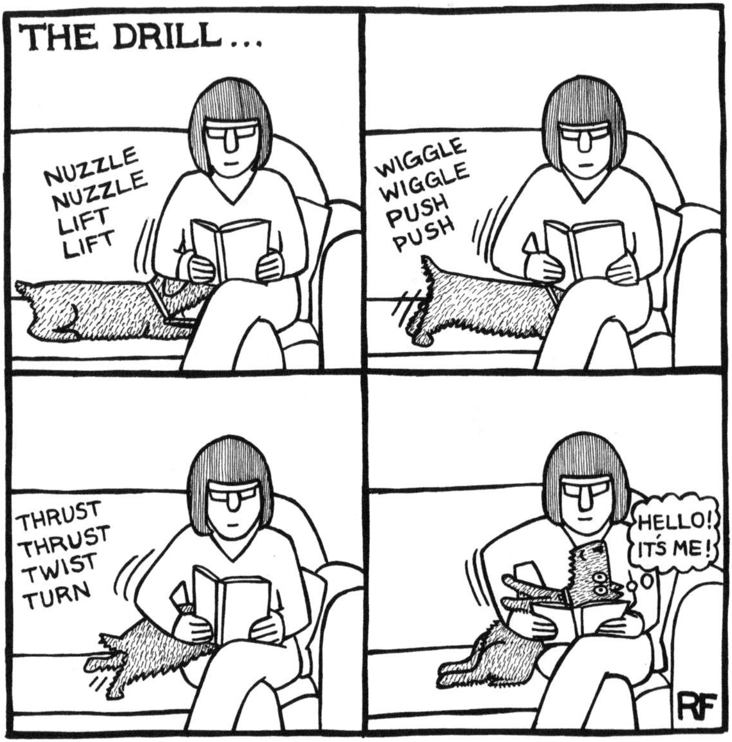
THE DRILL ...
NUZZLE
NUZZLE
LIFT
LIFT
WIGGLE
WIGGLE
PUSH
PUSH
THRUST
THRUST
TWIST
TURN
HELLO! IT'S ME!
RF

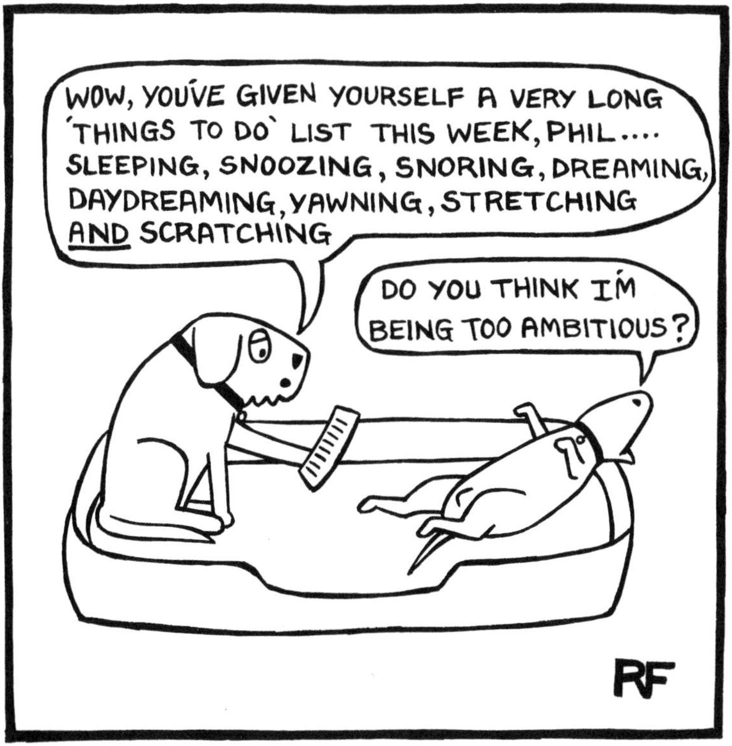
WOW, YOU'VE GIVEN YOURSELF A VERY LONG 'THINGS TO DO' LIST THIS WEEK, PHIL.... SLEEPING, SNOOZING, SNORING, DREAMING, DAYDREAMING, YAWNING, STRETCHING AND SCRATCHING
DO YOU THINK I'M BEING TOO AMBITIOUS?
RF

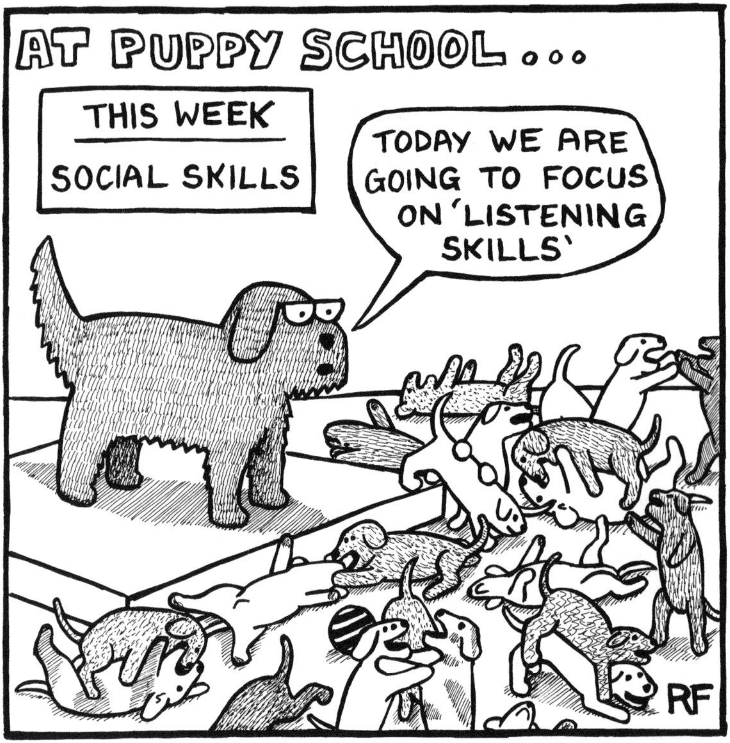
AT PUPPY SCHOOL...
THIS WEEK
SOCIAL SKILLS
TODAY WE ARE GOING TO FOCUS ON 'LISTENING SKILLS'
RF

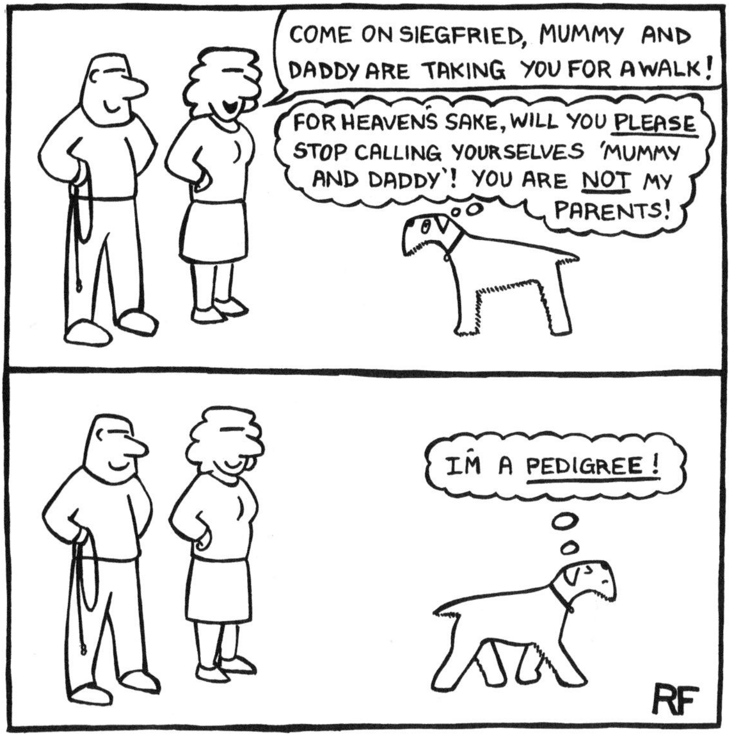
COME ON SIEGFRIED, MUMMY AND DADDY ARE TAKING YOU FOR A WALK!
FOR HEAVEN'S SAKE, WILL YOU PLEASE STOP CALLING YOURSELVES 'MUMMY AND DADDY'! YOU ARE NOT MY PARENTS!
I'M A PEDIGREE!
RF

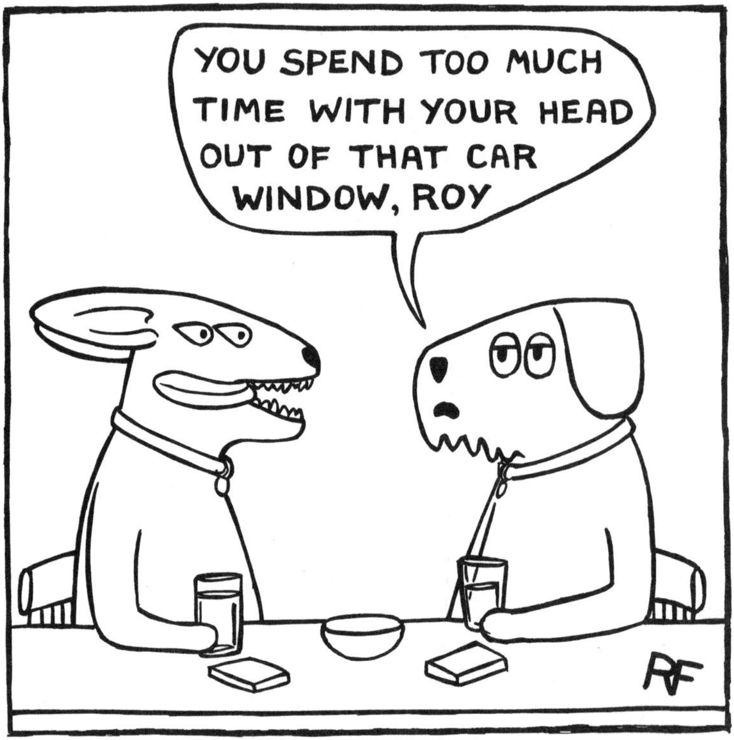
YOU SPEND TOO MUCH TIME WITH YOUR HEAD OUT OF THAT CAR WINDOW, ROY
RF

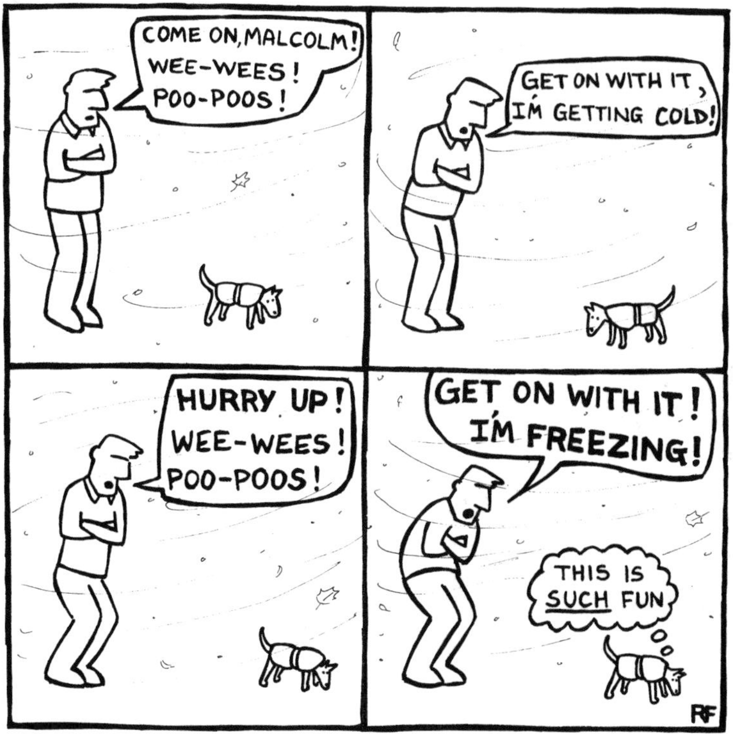
COME ON, MALCOLM! WEE-WEES! POO-POOS!
GET ON WITH IT, I'M GETTING COLD!
HURRY UP! WEE-WEES! POO-POOS!
GET ON WITH IT! I'M FREEZING!
THIS IS SUCH FUN
RF

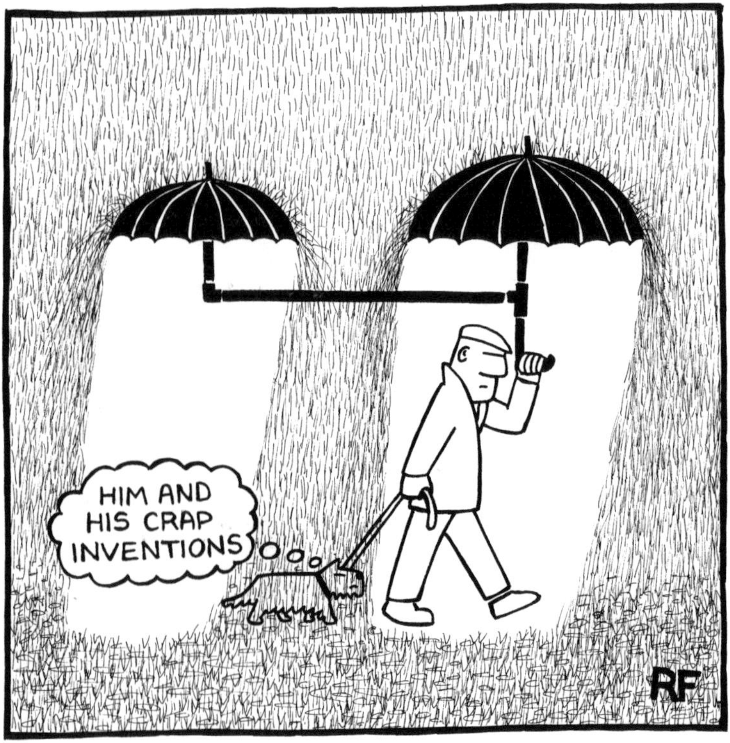
HIM AND
HIS CRAP
INVENTIONS
RF

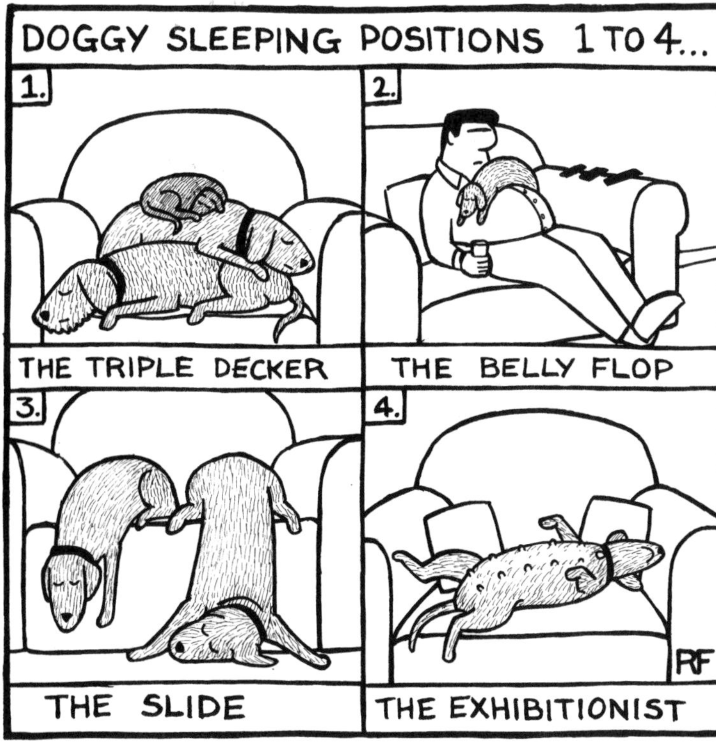
DOGGY SLEEPING POSITIONS 1 TO 4...
1.
THE TRIPLE DECKER
2.
THE BELLY FLOP
3.
THE SLIDE
4.
THE EXHIBITIONIST
RF

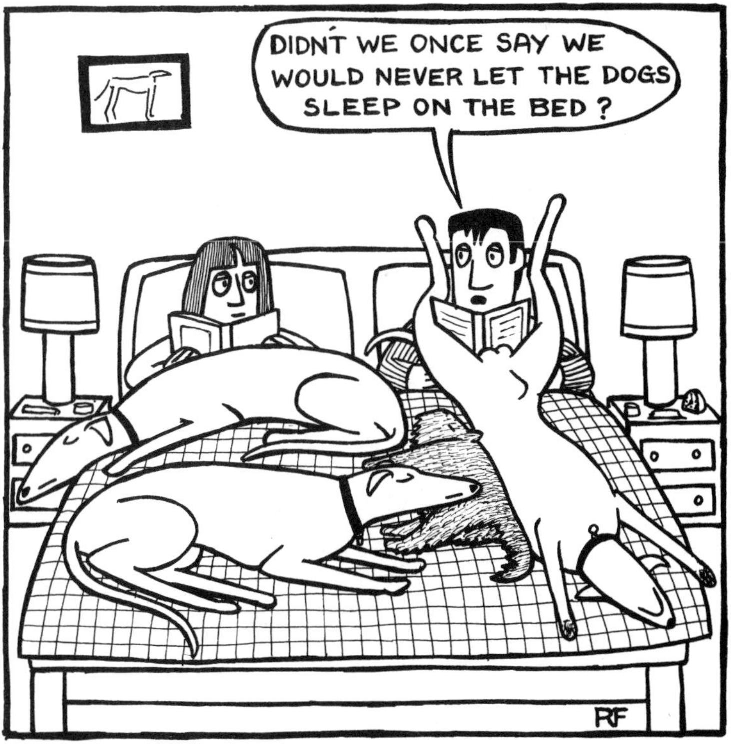
DIDN'T WE ONCE SAY WE WOULD NEVER LET THE DOGS SLEEP ON THE BED?
RF

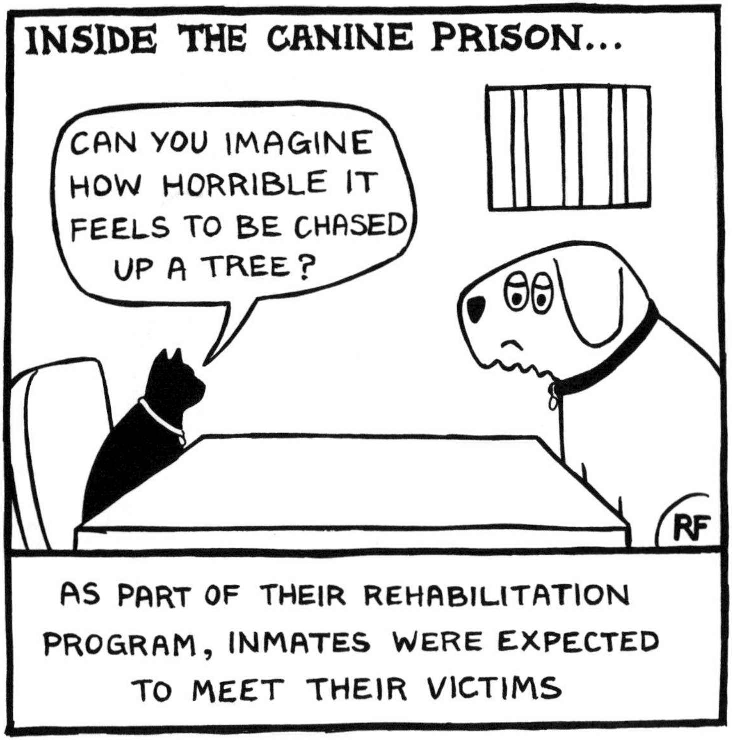
INSIDE THE CANINE PRISON...
CAN YOU IMAGINE HOW HORRIBLE IT FEELS TO BE CHASED UP A TREE?
RF
AS PART OF THEIR REHABILITATION PROGRAM, INMATES WERE EXPECTED TO MEET THEIR VICTIMS

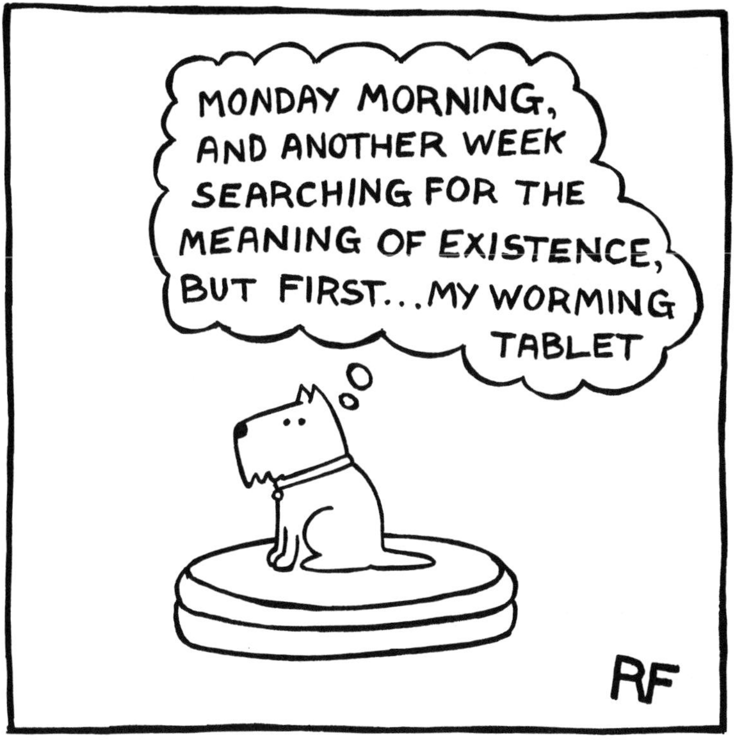
MONDAY MORNING, AND ANOTHER WEEK SEARCHING FOR THE MEANING OF EXISTENCE, BUT FIRST...MY WORMING TABLET
RF

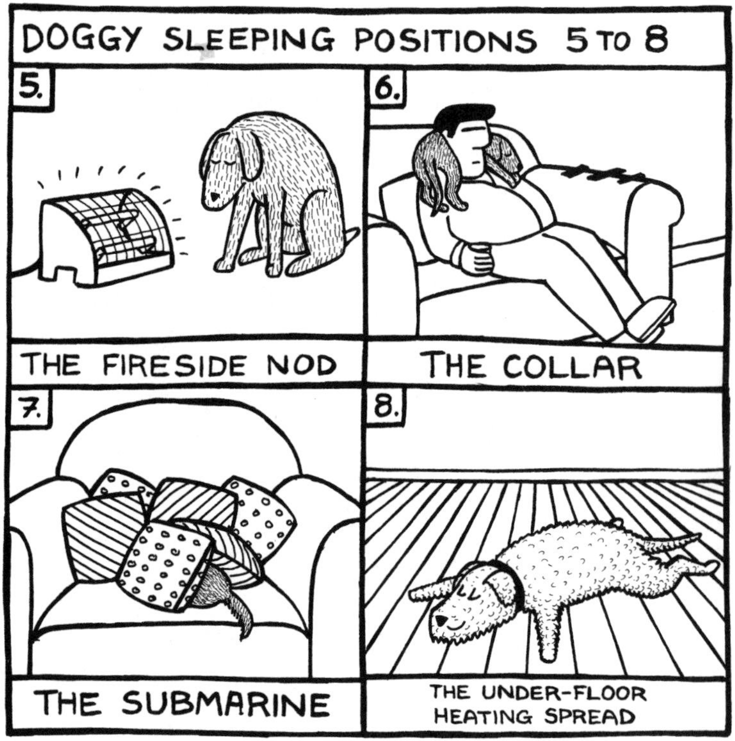
DOGGY SLEEPING POSITIONS 5 TO 8
5.
THE FIRESIDE NOD
6.
THE COLLAR
7.
THE SUBMARINE
8.
THE UNDER-FLOOR HEATING SPREAD

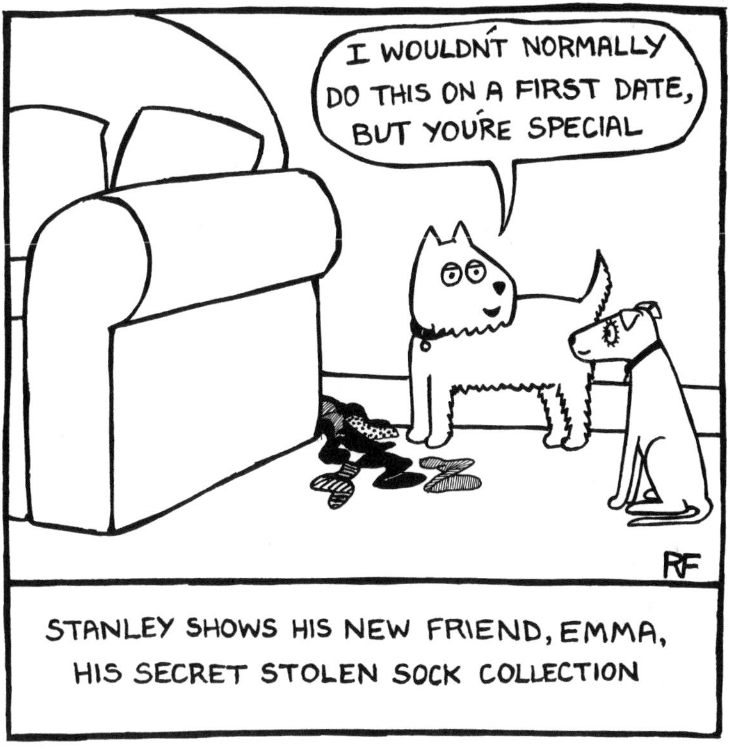
I WOULDN'T NORMALLY DO THIS ON A FIRST DATE, BUT YOU'RE SPECIAL
RF

STANLEY SHOWS HIS NEW FRIEND, EMMA, HIS SECRET STOLEN SOCK COLLECTION

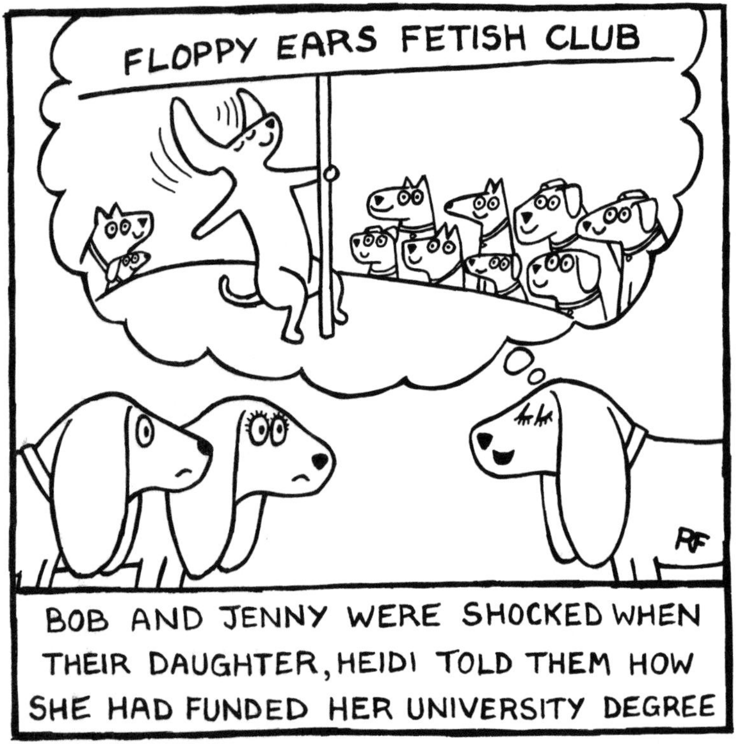
FLOPPY EARS FETISH CLUB
RF
BOB AND JENNY WERE SHOCKED WHEN THEIR DAUGHTER, HEIDI TOLD THEM HOW SHE HAD FUNDED HER UNIVERSITY DEGREE

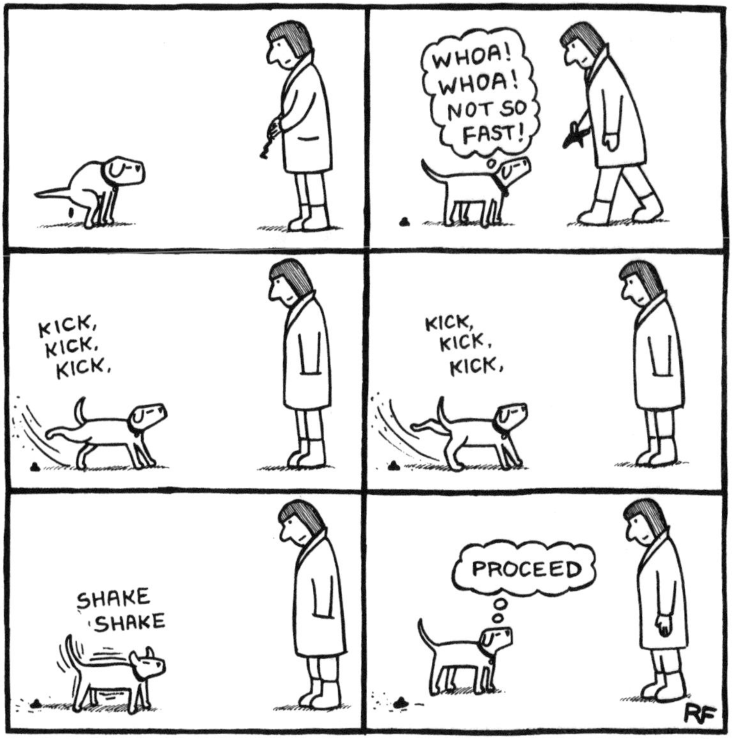
WHOA! WHOA! NOT SO FAST!
KICK, KICK, KICK,
KICK, KICK, KICK,
SHAKE SHAKE
PROCEED
RF

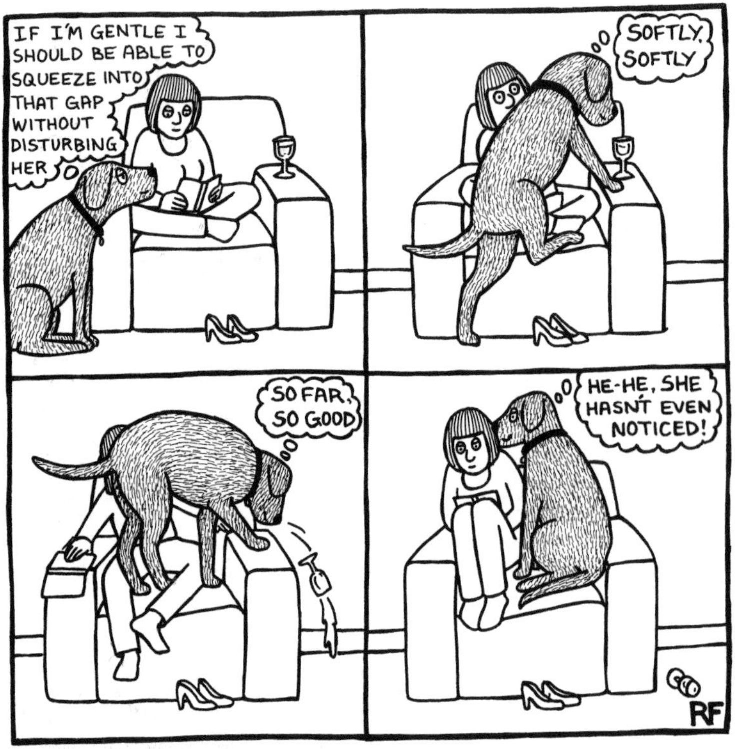
IF I'M GENTLE I SHOULD BE ABLE TO SQUEEZE INTO THAT GAP WITHOUT DISTURBING HER
SOFTLY, SOFTLY
SO FAR, SO GOOD
HE-HE, SHE HASN'T EVEN NOTICED!
RF

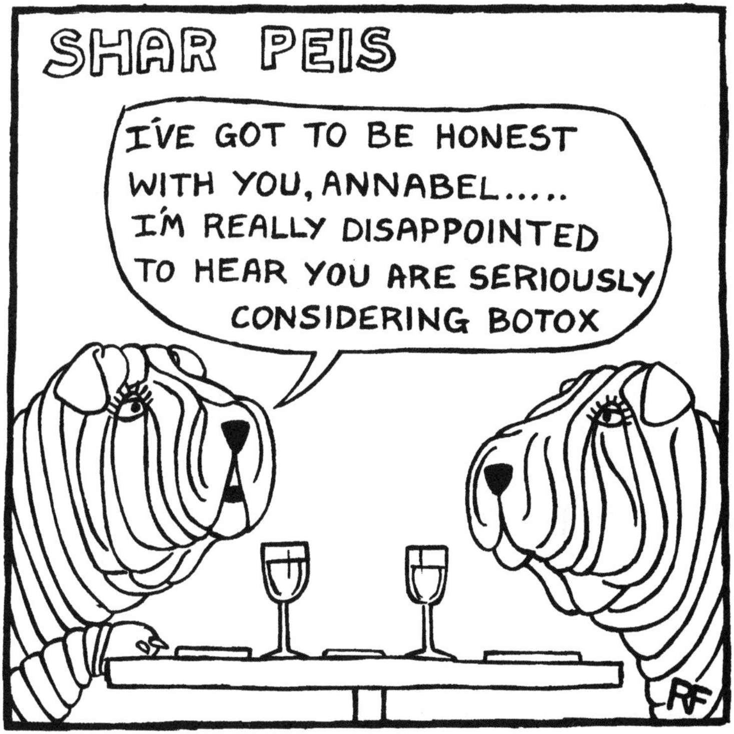
SHAR PEIS
I'VE GOT TO BE HONEST WITH YOU, ANNABEL..... I'M REALLY DISAPPOINTED TO HEAR YOU ARE SERIOUSLY CONSIDERING BOTOX
RF

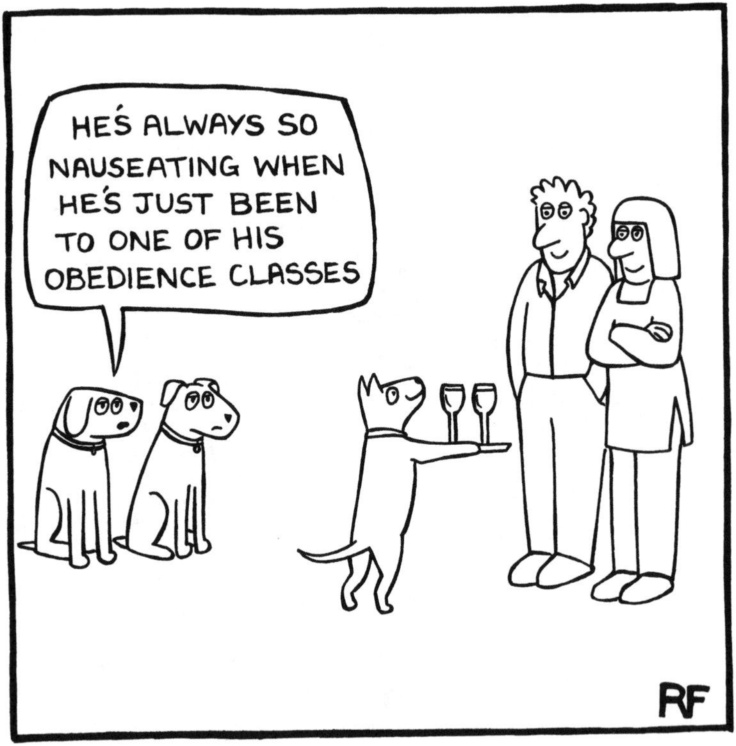
HE'S ALWAYS SO NAUSEATING WHEN HE'S JUST BEEN TO ONE OF HIS OBEDIENCE CLASSES
RF

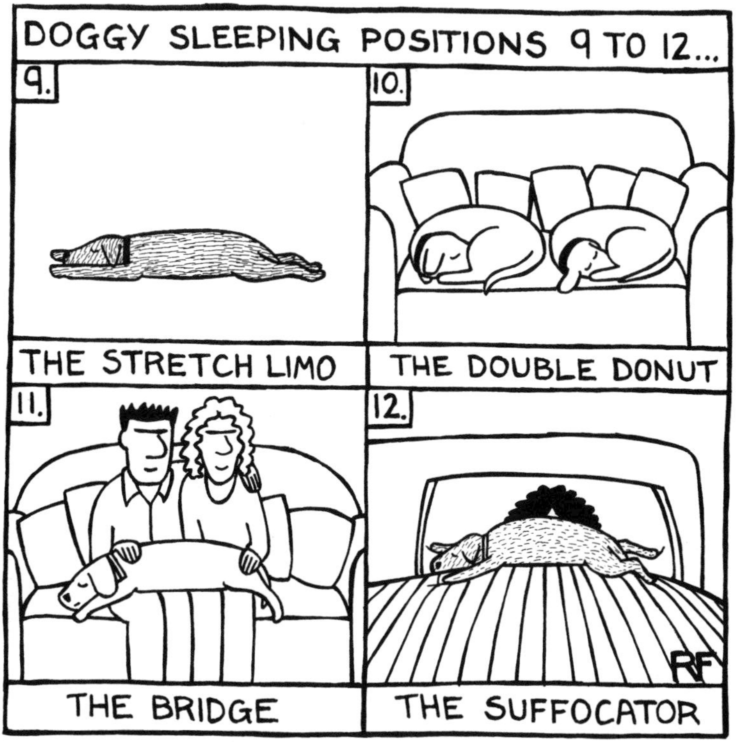
DOGGY SLEEPING POSITIONS 9 TO 12...
9.
THE STRETCH LIMO
10.
THE DOUBLE DONUT
11.
THE BRIDGE
12.
THE SUFFOCATOR
RF

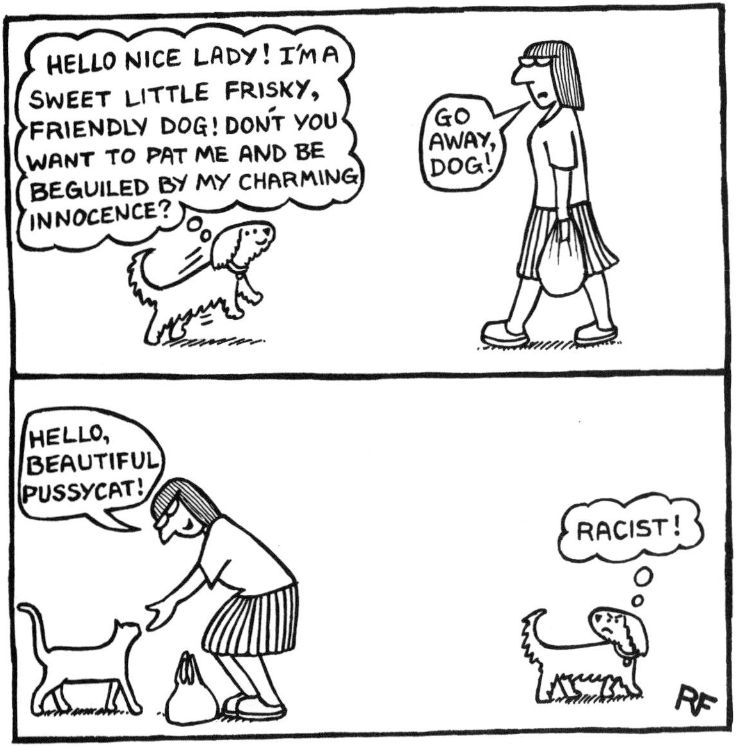
HELLO NICE LADY! I'M A SWEET LITTLE FRISKY, FRIENDLY DOG! DON'T YOU WANT TO PAT ME AND BE BEGUILED BY MY CHARMING INNOCENCE?
GO AWAY, DOG!
HELLO, BEAUTIFUL PUSSYCAT!
RACIST!
RF

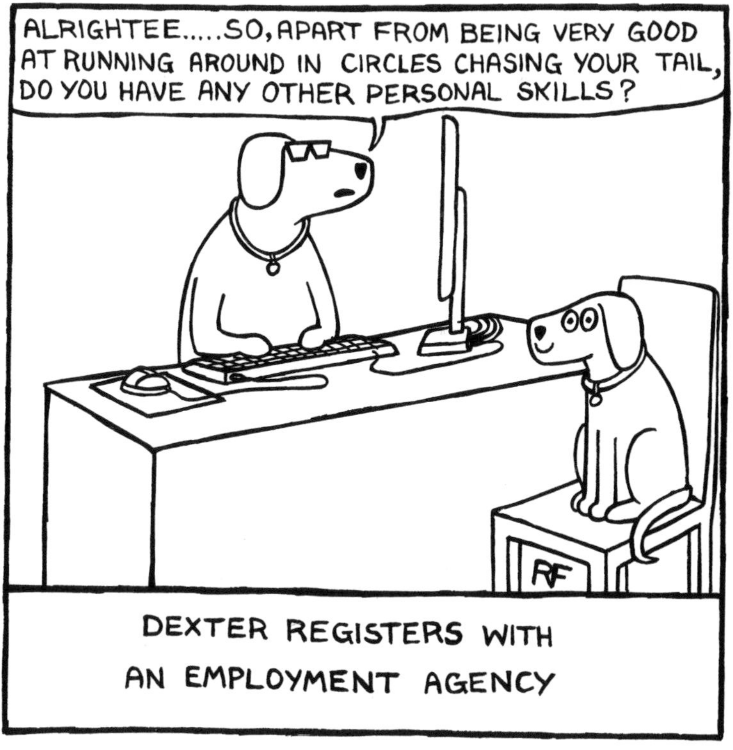
ALRIGHTEE.....SO, APART FROM BEING VERY GOOD AT RUNNING AROUND IN CIRCLES CHASING YOUR TAIL, DO YOU HAVE ANY OTHER PERSONAL SKILLS?

DEXTER REGISTERS WITH AN EMPLOYMENT AGENCY

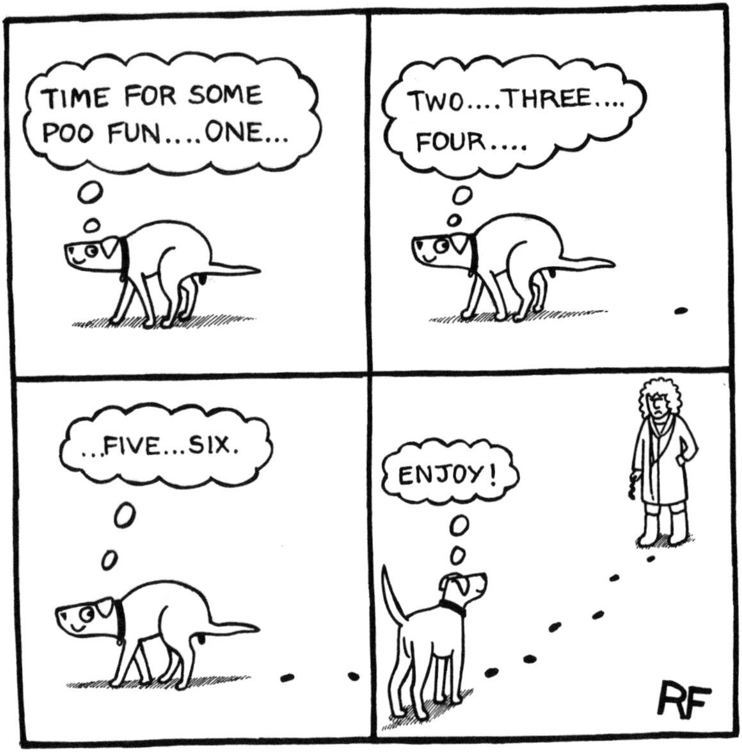
TIME FOR SOME POO FUN....ONE...
TWO....THREE....
FOUR....
...FIVE...SIX.
ENJOY!
RF

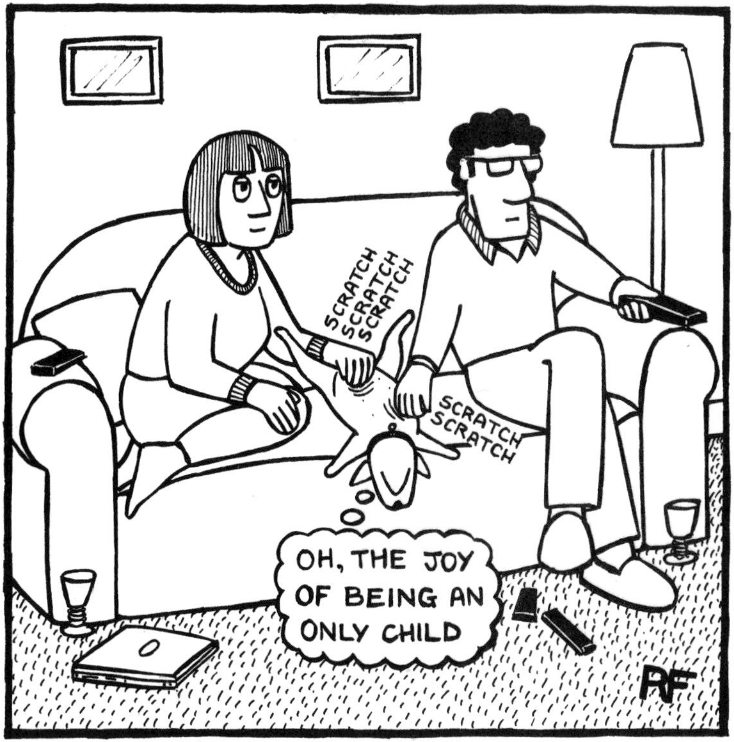
SCRATCH
SCRATCH
SCRATCH
SCRATCH
SCRATCH
OH, THE JOY OF BEING AN ONLY CHILD
RF

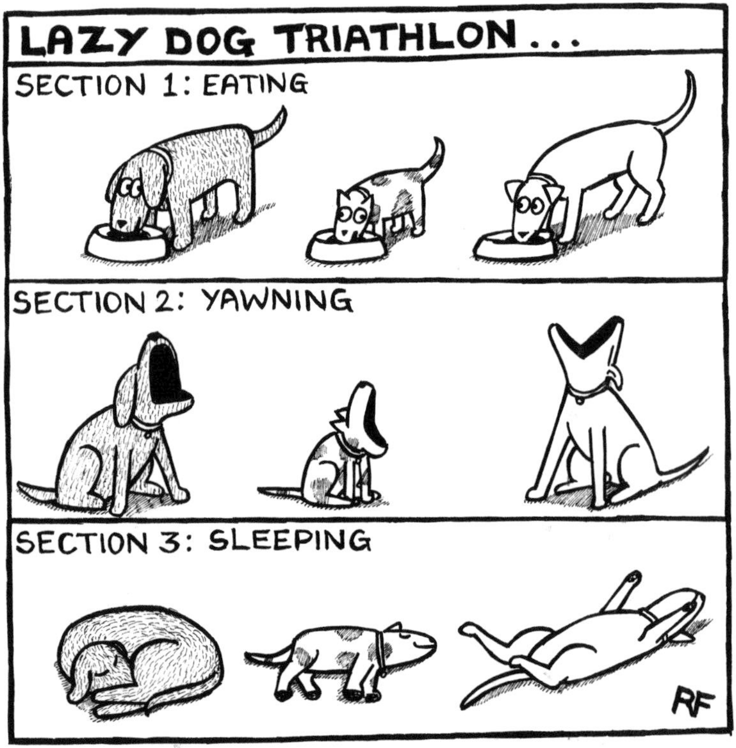
LAZY DOG TRIATHLON...
SECTION 1: EATING
SECTION 2: YAWNING
SECTION 3: SLEEPING
RF

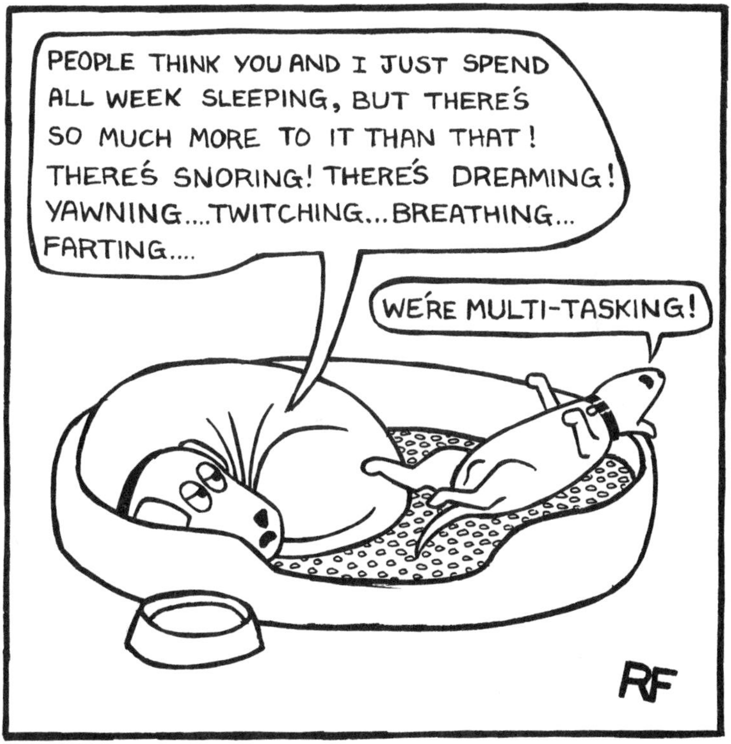
PEOPLE THINK YOU AND I JUST SPEND ALL WEEK SLEEPING, BUT THERE'S SO MUCH MORE TO IT THAN THAT! THERE'S SNORING! THERE'S DREAMING! YAWNING....TWITCHING...BREATHING... FARTING....
WE'RE MULTI-TASKING!
RF

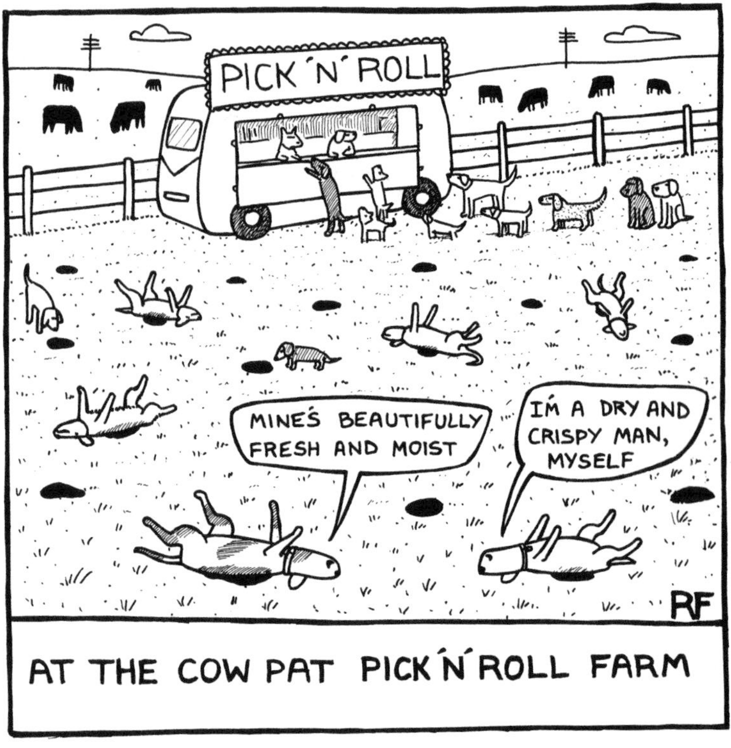
PICK 'N' ROLL
MINE'S BEAUTIFULLY FRESH AND MOIST
I'M A DRY AND CRISPY MAN, MYSELF
RF

AT THE COW PAT PICK 'N' ROLL FARM

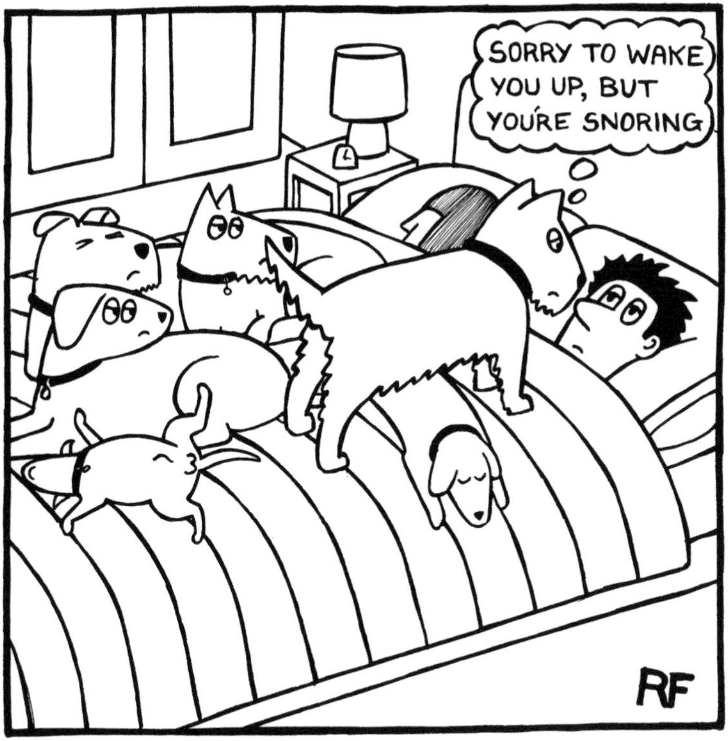
SORRY TO WAKE YOU UP, BUT YOU'RE SNORING
RF

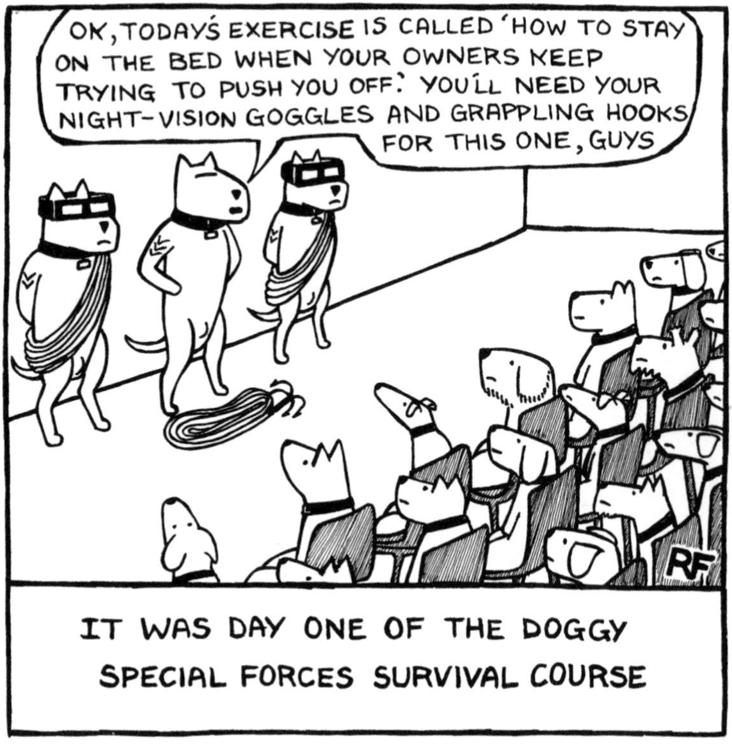
OK, TODAY'S EXERCISE IS CALLED 'HOW TO STAY ON THE BED WHEN YOUR OWNERS KEEP TRYING TO PUSH YOU OFF.' YOU'LL NEED YOUR NIGHT-VISION GOGGLES AND GRAPPLING HOOKS FOR THIS ONE, GUYS
RF

IT WAS DAY ONE OF THE DOGGY SPECIAL FORCES SURVIVAL COURSE

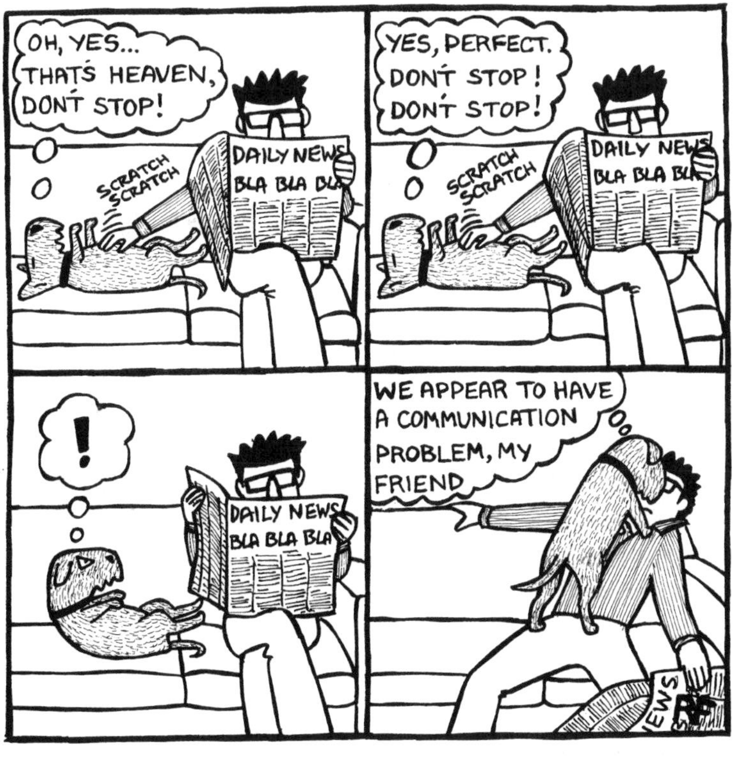
OH, YES...
THAT'S HEAVEN,
DON'T STOP!
DAILY NEWS
BLA BLA BLA
SCRATCH SCRATCH
YES, PERFECT.
DON'T STOP!
DON'T STOP!
DAILY NEWS
BLA BLA BLA
SCRATCH SCRATCH
!
DAILY NEWS
BLA BLA BLA
WE APPEAR TO HAVE
A COMMUNICATION
PROBLEM, MY
FRIEND
NEWS

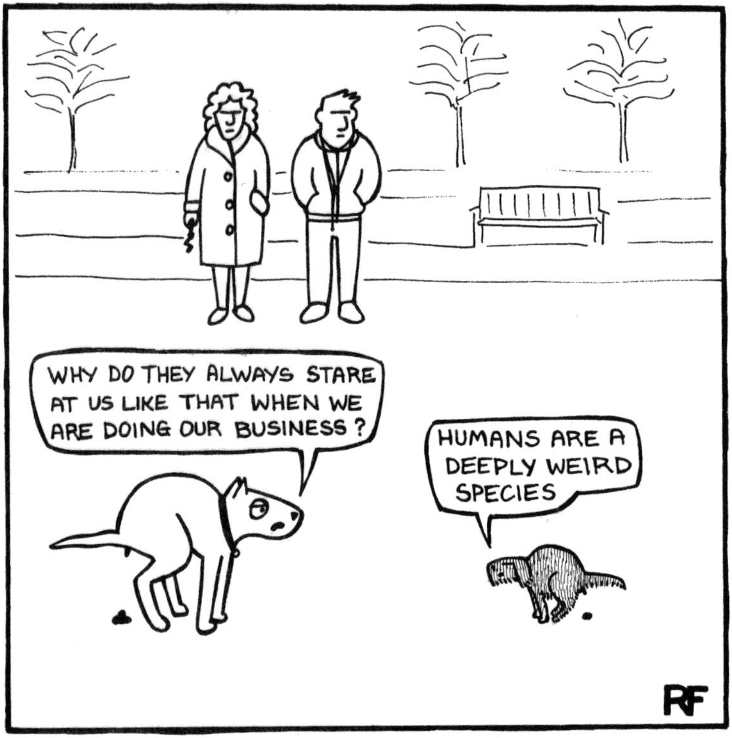
WHY DO THEY ALWAYS STARE AT US LIKE THAT WHEN WE ARE DOING OUR BUSINESS?
HUMANS ARE A DEEPLY WEIRD SPECIES
RF

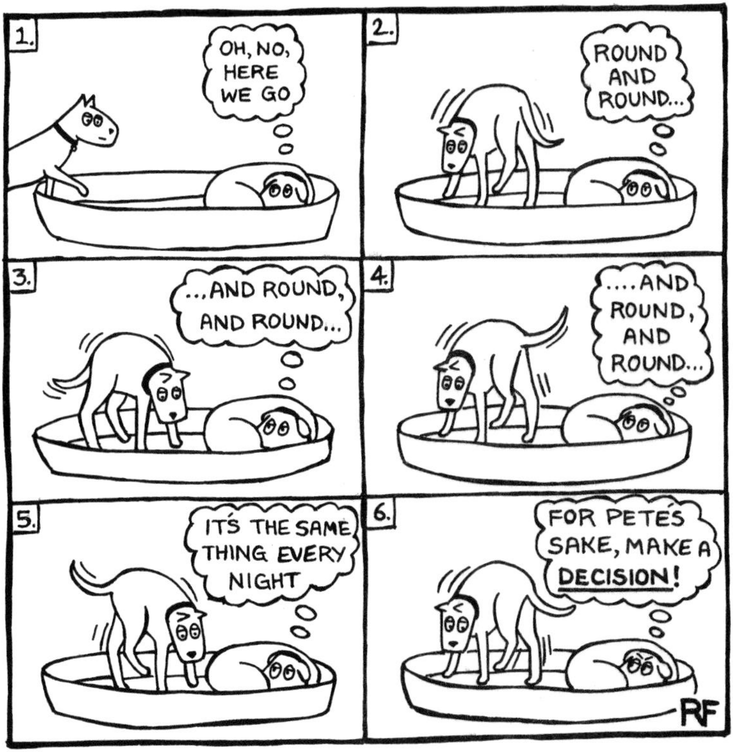
1.
OH, NO, HERE WE GO
2.
ROUND AND ROUND...
3.
..., AND ROUND, AND ROUND...
4.
.....AND ROUND, AND ROUND...
5.
IT'S THE SAME THING EVERY NIGHT
6.
FOR PETE'S SAKE, MAKE A DECISION!
RF

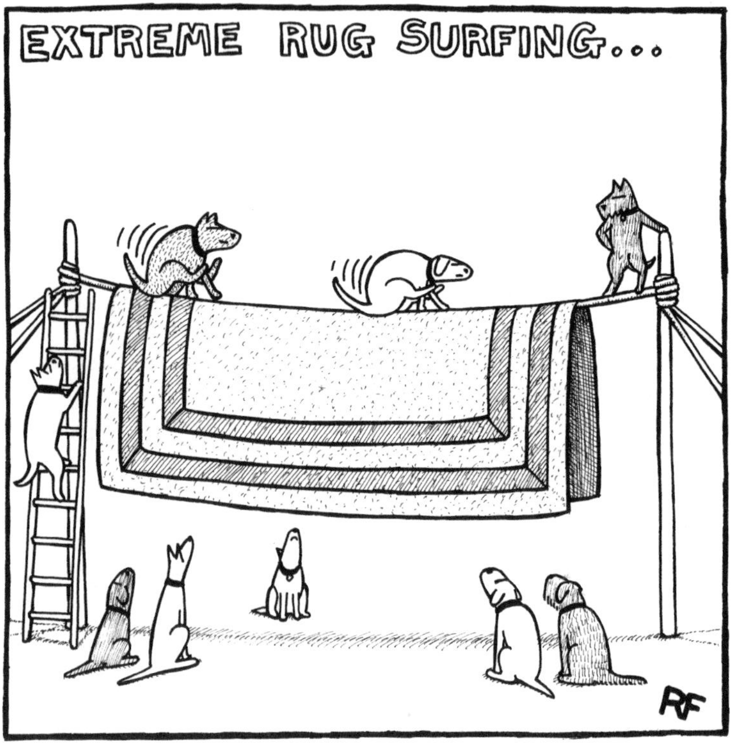
EXTREME RUG SURFING...
RF

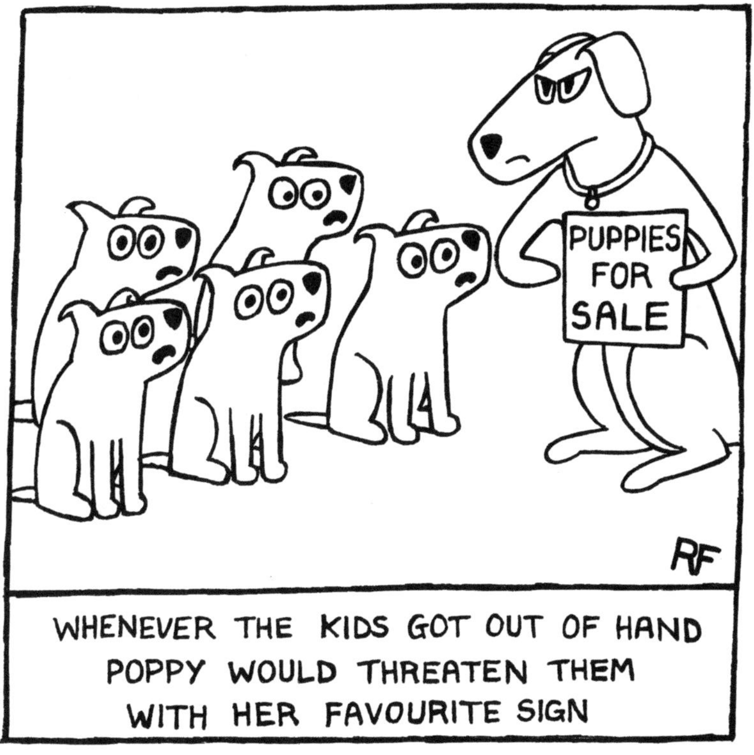
PUPPIES FOR SALE
RF

WHENEVER THE KIDS GOT OUT OF HAND POPPY WOULD THREATEN THEM WITH HER FAVOURITE SIGN

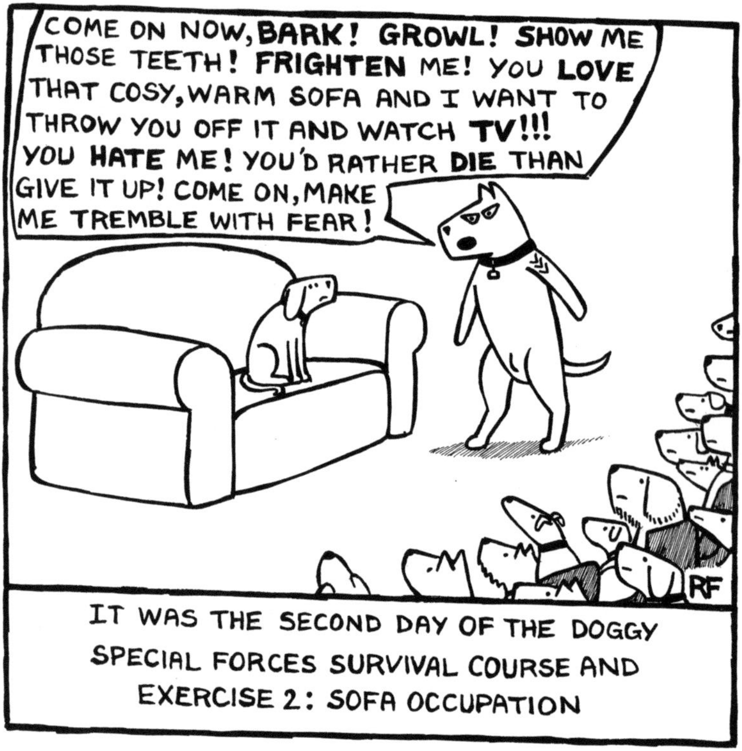
COME ON NOW, BARK! GROWL! SHOW ME THOSE TEETH! FRIGHTEN ME! YOU LOVE THAT COSY, WARM SOFA AND I WANT TO THROW YOU OFF IT AND WATCH TV!!! YOU HATE ME! YOU'D RATHER DIE THAN GIVE IT UP! COME ON, MAKE ME TREMBLE WITH FEAR!
RF
IT WAS THE SECOND DAY OF THE DOGGY SPECIAL FORCES SURVIVAL COURSE AND EXERCISE 2: SOFA OCCUPATION

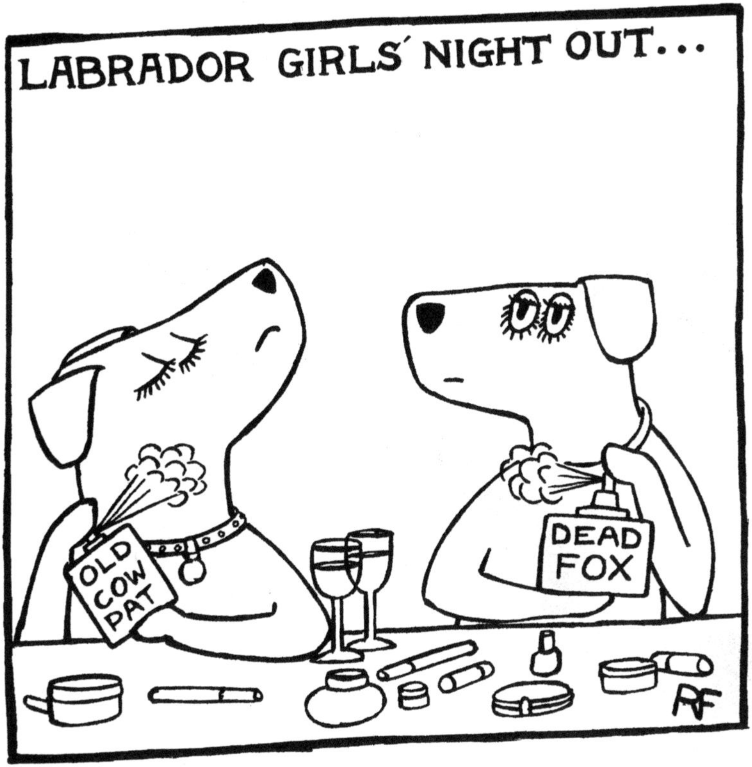
LABRADOR GIRLS' NIGHT OUT...
OLD COW PAT
DEAD FOX
RF

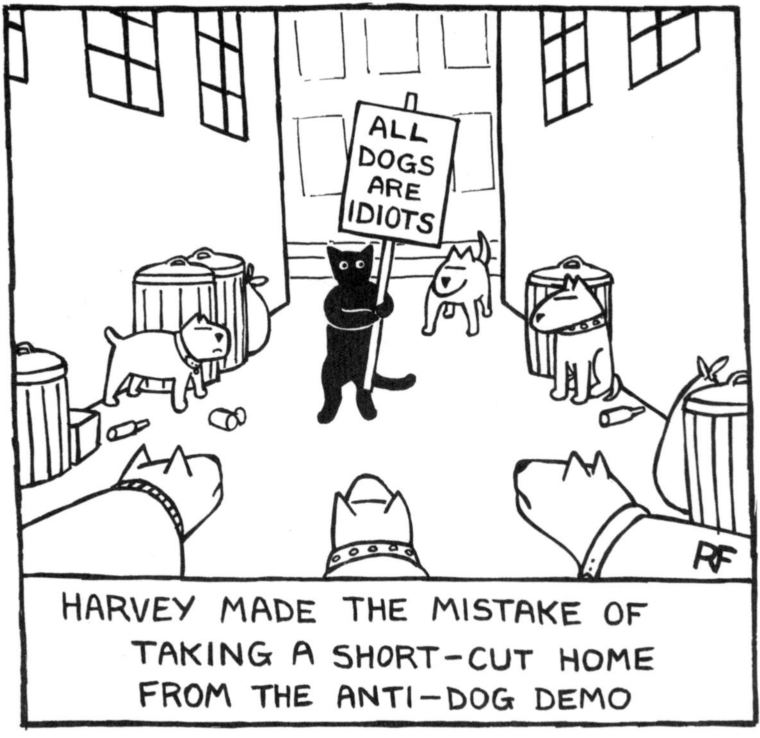
ALL DOGS ARE IDIOTS
RF

HARVEY MADE THE MISTAKE OF TAKING A SHORT-CUT HOME FROM THE ANTI-DOG DEMO

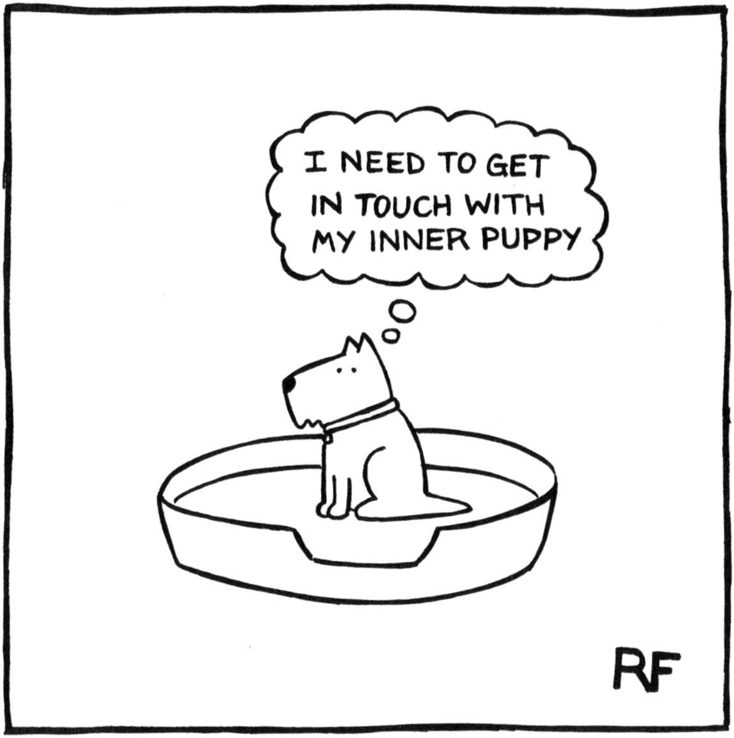
I NEED TO GET IN TOUCH WITH MY INNER PUPPY
RF

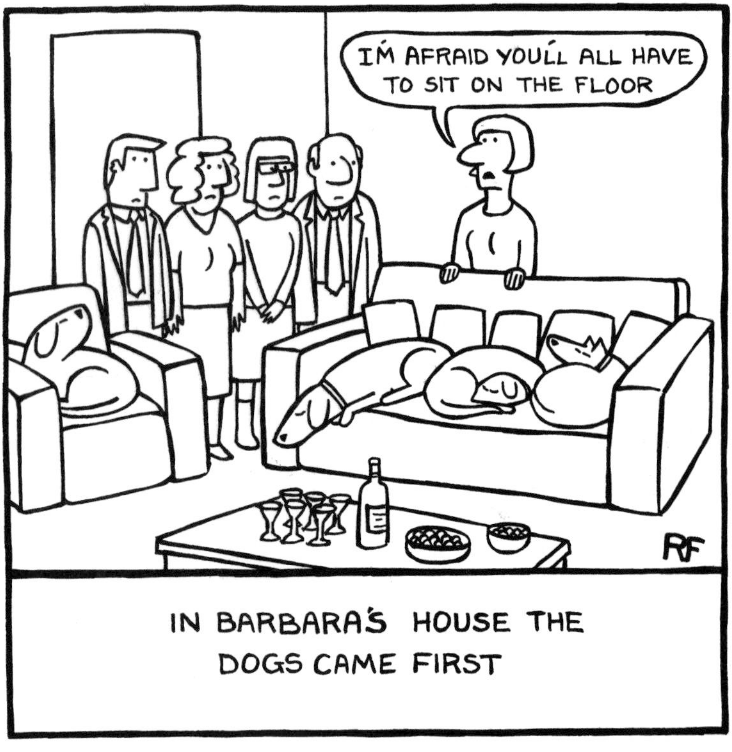
I'M AFRAID YOU'LL ALL HAVE TO SIT ON THE FLOOR
RF

IN BARBARA'S HOUSE THE DOGS CAME FIRST

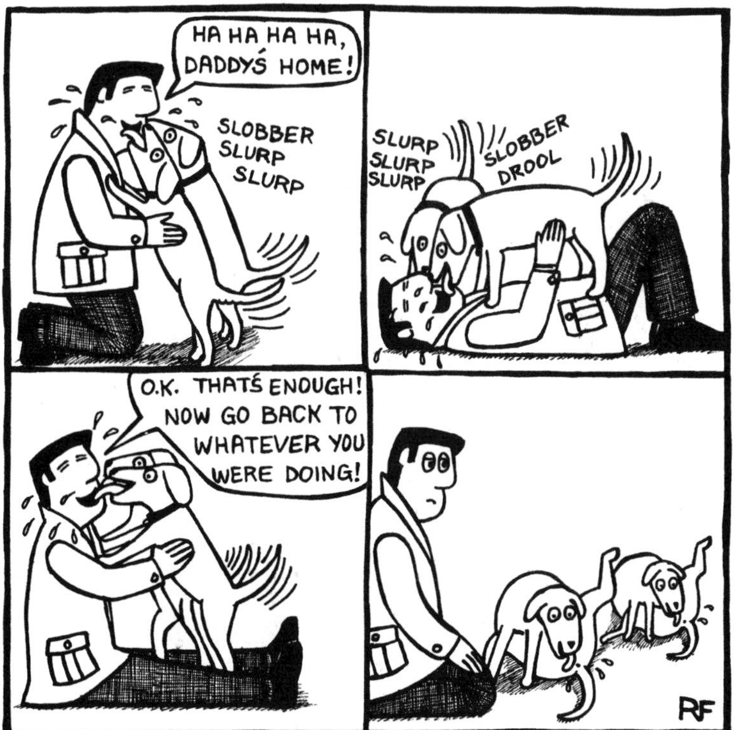
HA HA HA HA, DADDY'S HOME!
SLOBBER SLURP SLURP
SLURP SLURP SLURP
SLOBBER DROOL
O.K. THAT'S ENOUGH! NOW GO BACK TO WHATEVER YOU WERE DOING!
RF

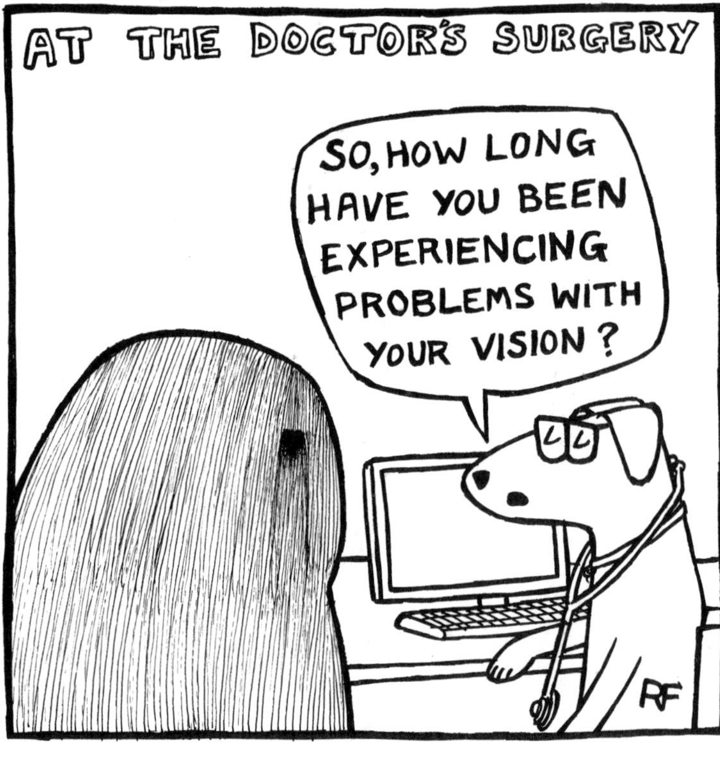
AT THE DOCTOR'S SURGERY
SO, HOW LONG HAVE YOU BEEN EXPERIENCING PROBLEMS WITH YOUR VISION?
RF

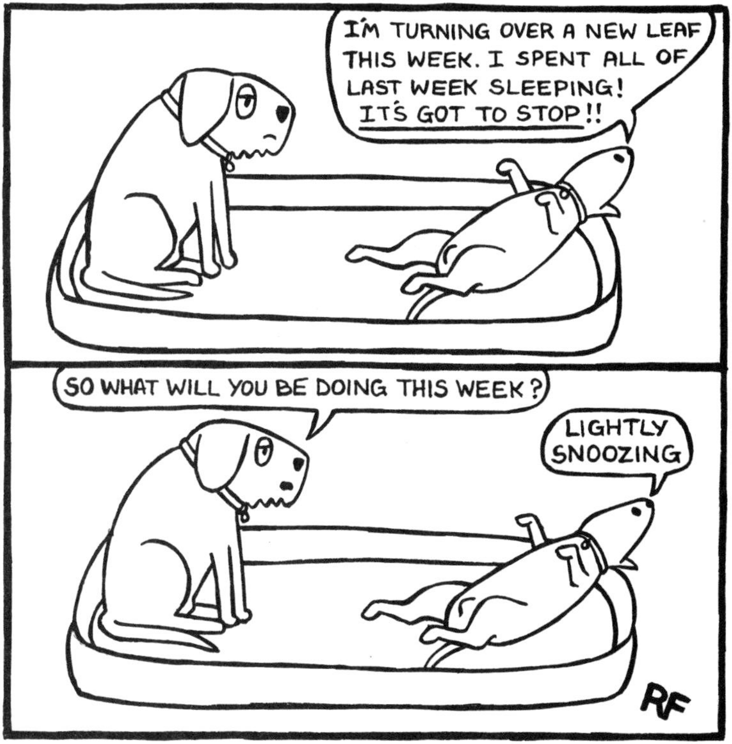
I'M TURNING OVER A NEW LEAF THIS WEEK. I SPENT ALL OF LAST WEEK SLEEPING! IT'S GOT TO STOP!!
SO WHAT WILL YOU BE DOING THIS WEEK?
LIGHTLY SNOOZING
RF

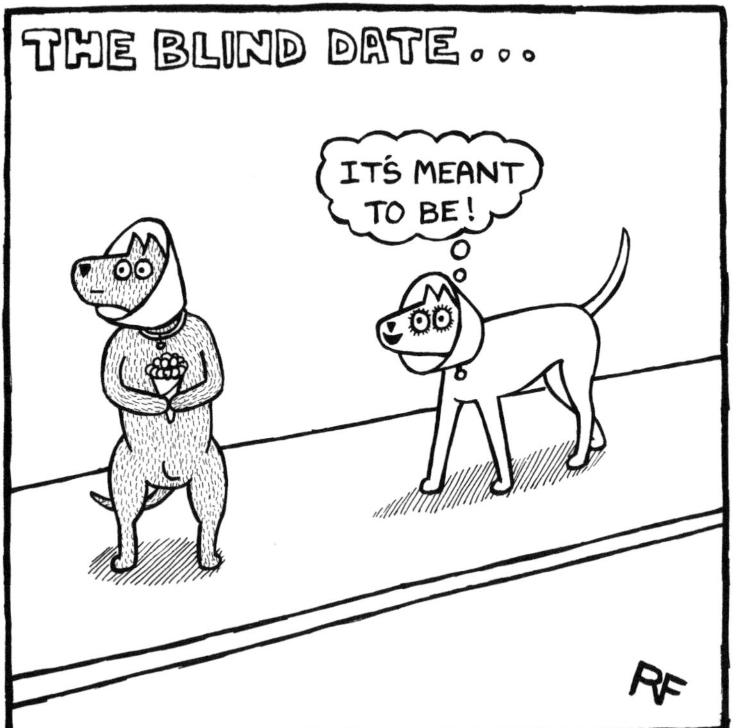
THE BLIND DATE...
ITS MEANT TO BE!
RF

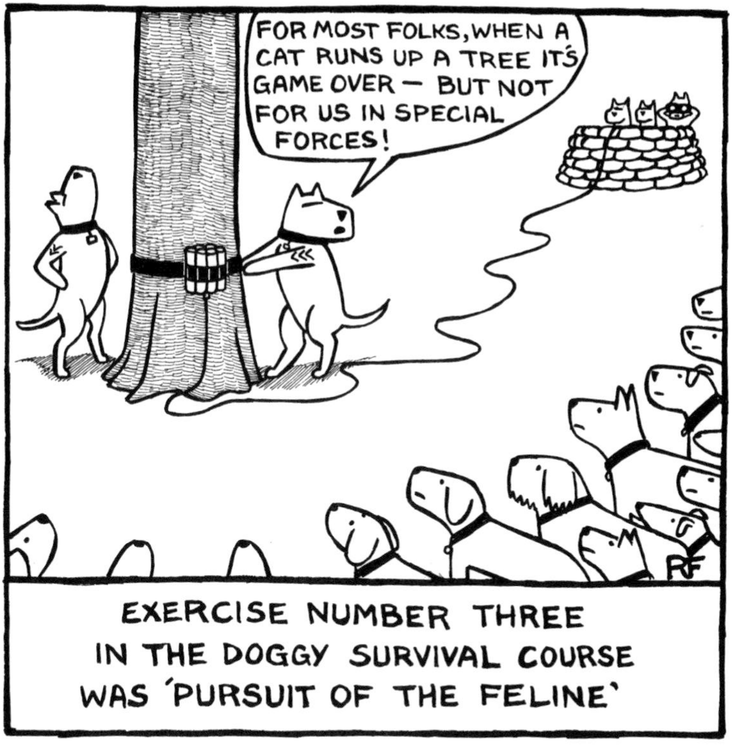
FOR MOST FOLKS, WHEN A CAT RUNS UP A TREE IT'S GAME OVER — BUT NOT FOR US IN SPECIAL FORCES!
RF

EXERCISE NUMBER THREE IN THE DOGGY SURVIVAL COURSE WAS 'PURSUIT OF THE FELINE'

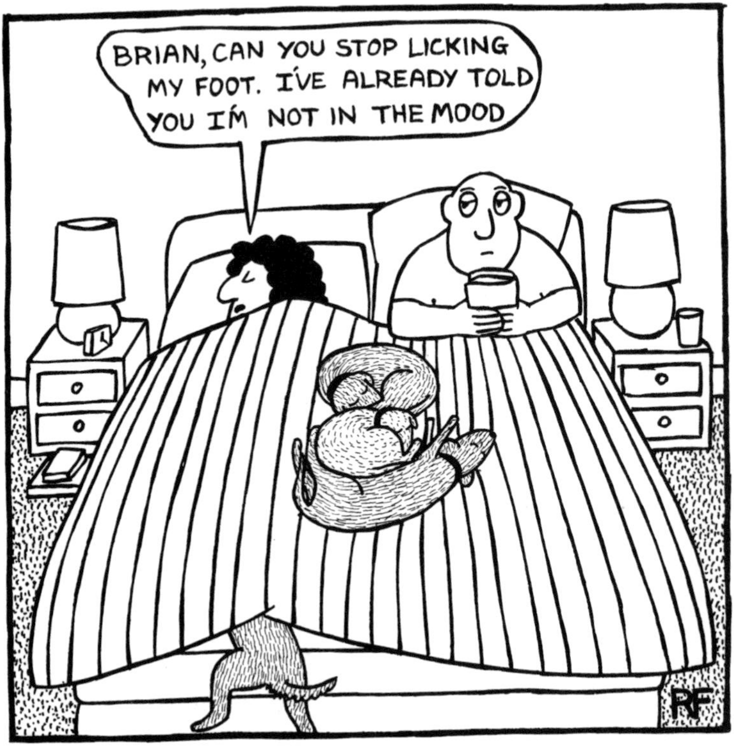
BRIAN, CAN YOU STOP LICKING MY FOOT. I'VE ALREADY TOLD YOU I'M NOT IN THE MOOD
RF

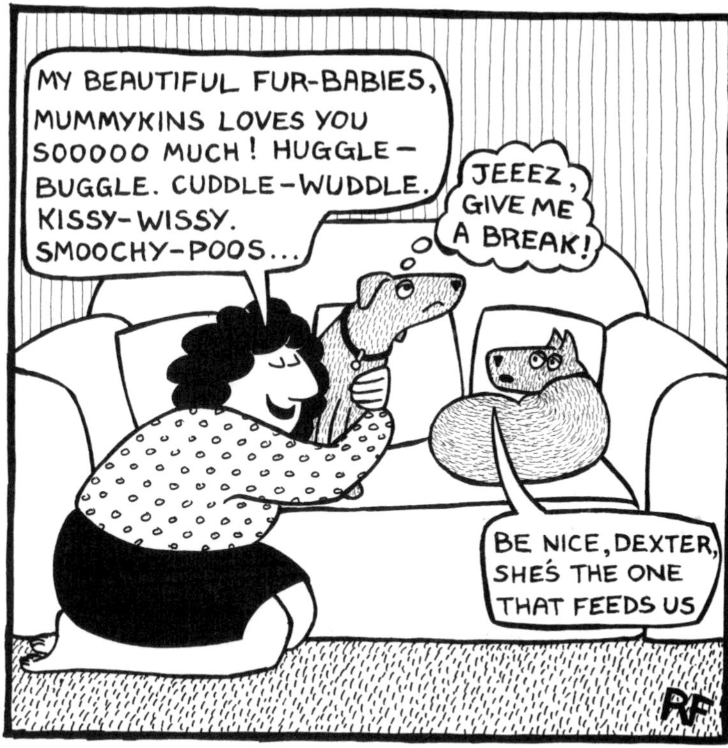
MY BEAUTIFUL FUR-BABIES, MUMMYKINS LOVES YOU SOOOOO MUCH! HUGGLE-BUGGLE. CUDDLE-WUDDLE. KISSY-WISSY. SMOOCHY-POOS...
JEEEZ, GIVE ME A BREAK!
BE NICE, DEXTER, SHE'S THE ONE THAT FEEDS US
RF

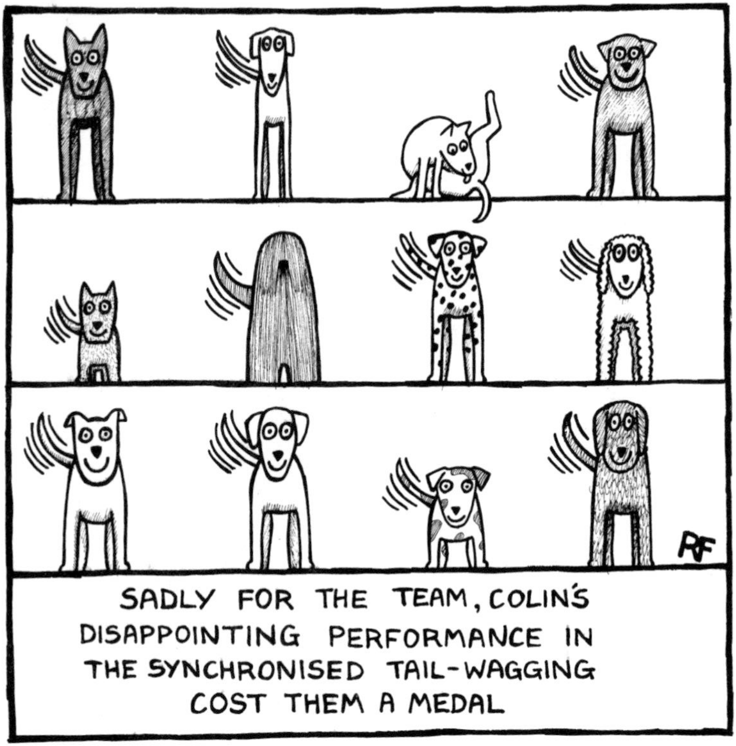
RF

SADLY FOR THE TEAM, COLIN'S DISAPPOINTING PERFORMANCE IN THE SYNCHRONISED TAIL-WAGGING COST THEM A MEDAL

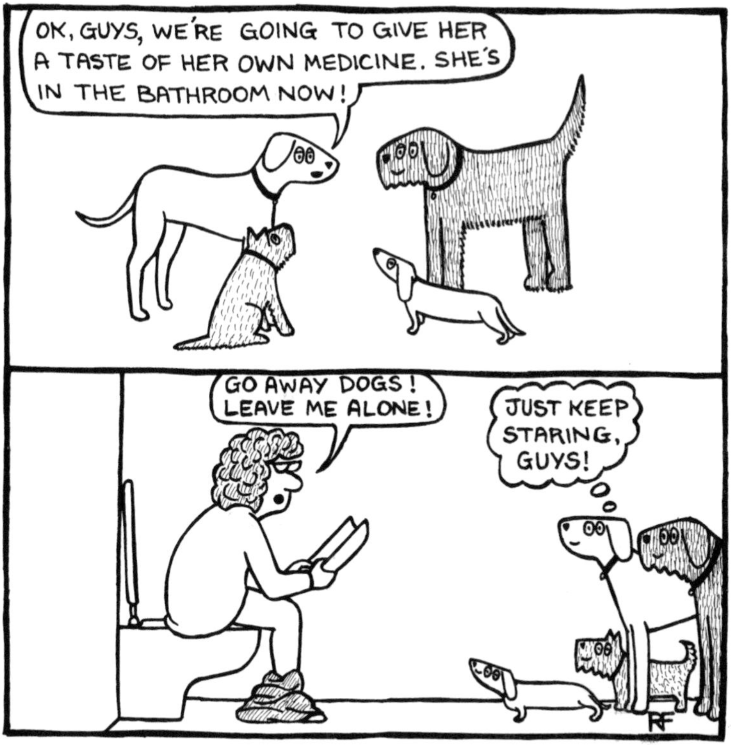
OK, GUYS, WE'RE GOING TO GIVE HER A TASTE OF HER OWN MEDICINE. SHE'S IN THE BATHROOM NOW!
GO AWAY DOGS! LEAVE ME ALONE!
JUST KEEP STARING, GUYS!
RF

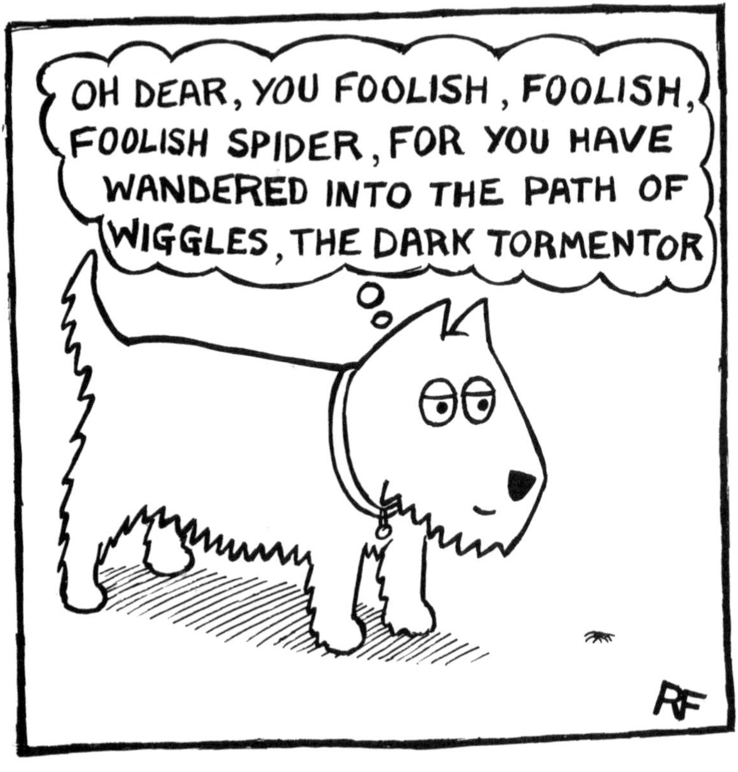
OH DEAR, YOU FOOLISH, FOOLISH, FOOLISH SPIDER, FOR YOU HAVE WANDERED INTO THE PATH OF WIGGLES, THE DARK TORMENTOR
RF

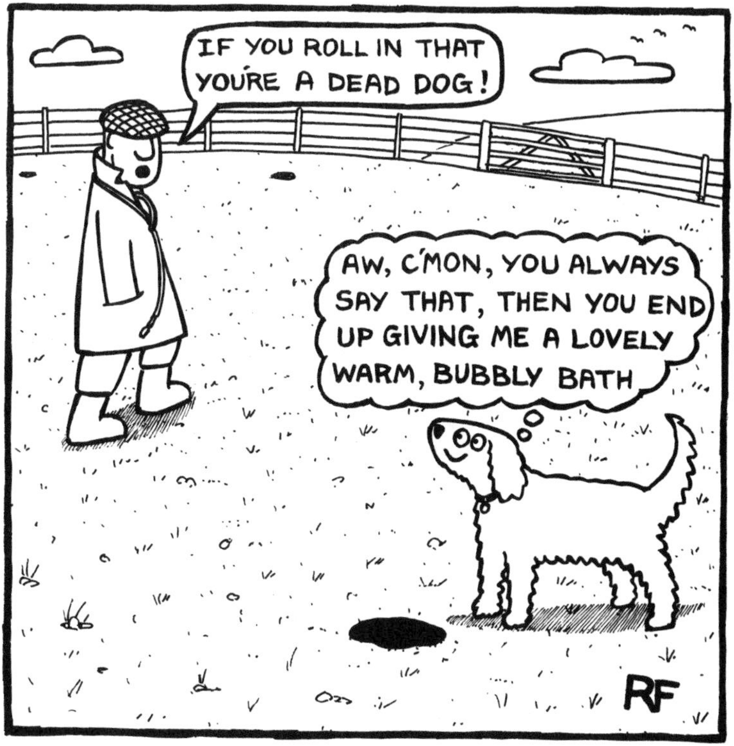
IF YOU ROLL IN THAT YOU'RE A DEAD DOG!
AW, C'MON, YOU ALWAYS SAY THAT, THEN YOU END UP GIVING ME A LOVELY WARM, BUBBLY BATH
RF

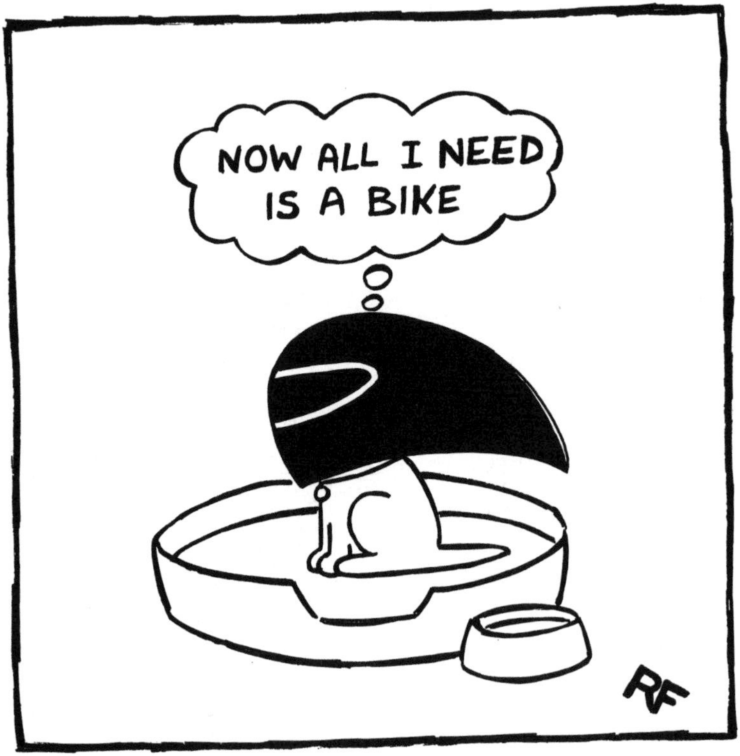
NOW ALL I NEED IS A BIKE
RF

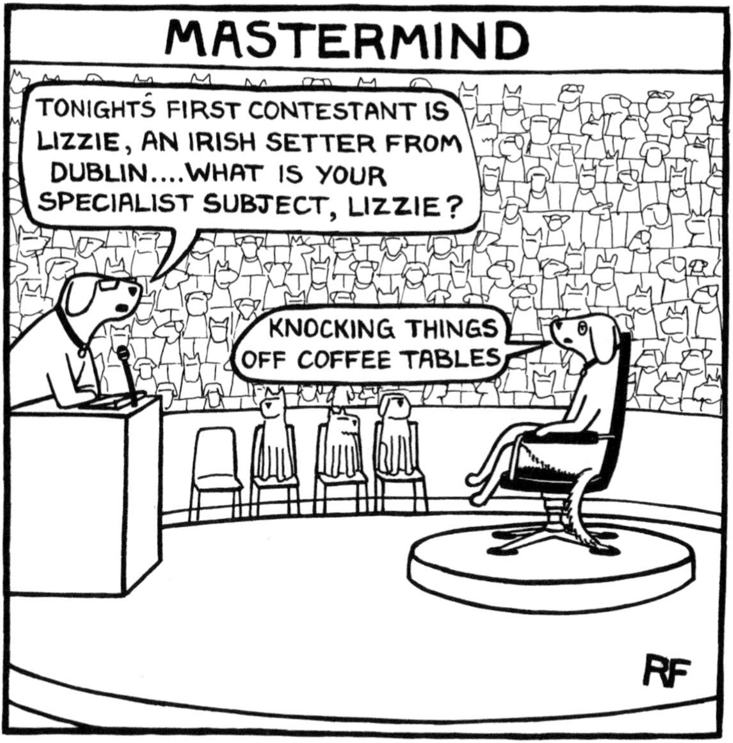
MASTERMIND
TONIGHTS FIRST CONTESTANT IS LIZZIE, AN IRISH SETTER FROM DUBLIN....WHAT IS YOUR SPECIALIST SUBJECT, LIZZIE?
KNOCKING THINGS OFF COFFEE TABLES
RF

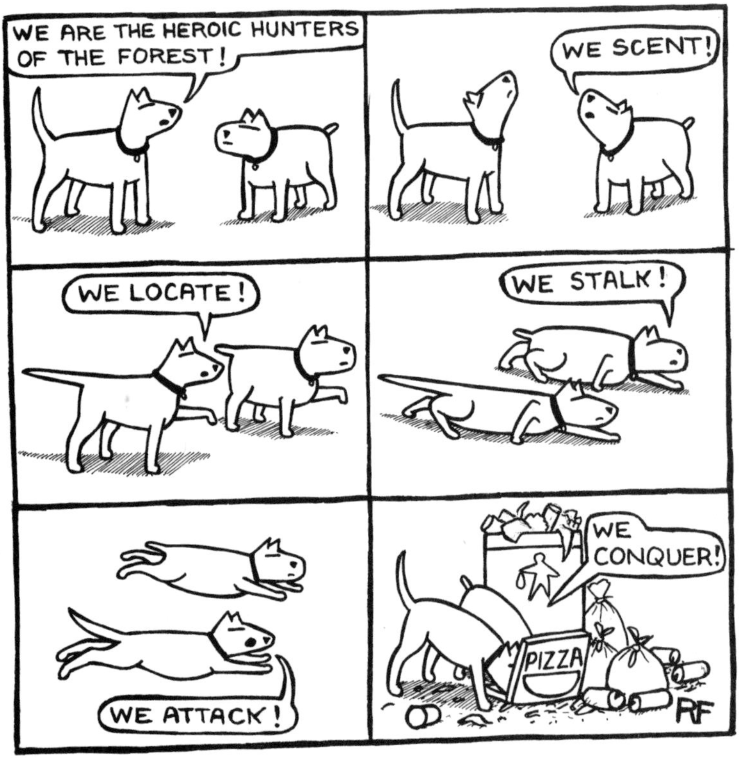
WE ARE THE HEROIC HUNTERS OF THE FOREST!
WE SCENT!
WE LOCATE!
WE STALK!
WE ATTACK!
PIZZA
WE CONQUER!
RF

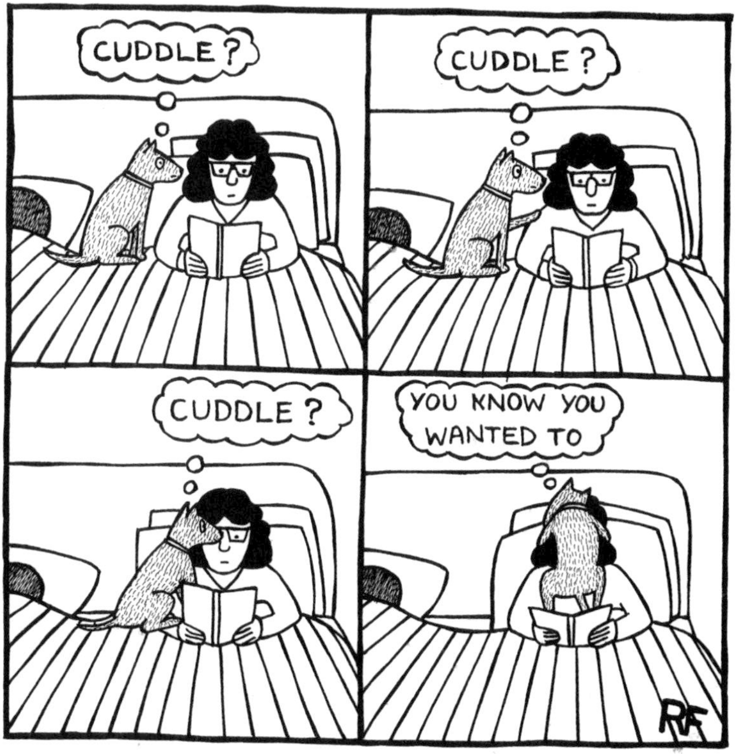
CUDDLE?
CUDDLE?
CUDDLE?
YOU KNOW YOU WANTED TO
RF

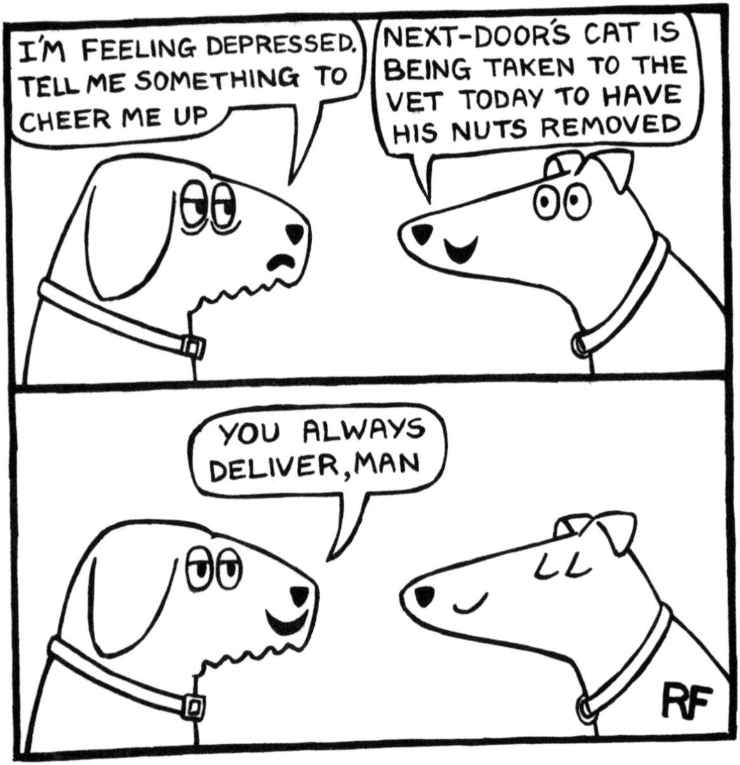
I'M FEELING DEPRESSED. TELL ME SOMETHING TO CHEER ME UP
NEXT-DOOR'S CAT IS BEING TAKEN TO THE VET TODAY TO HAVE HIS NUTS REMOVED
YOU ALWAYS DELIVER, MAN
RF

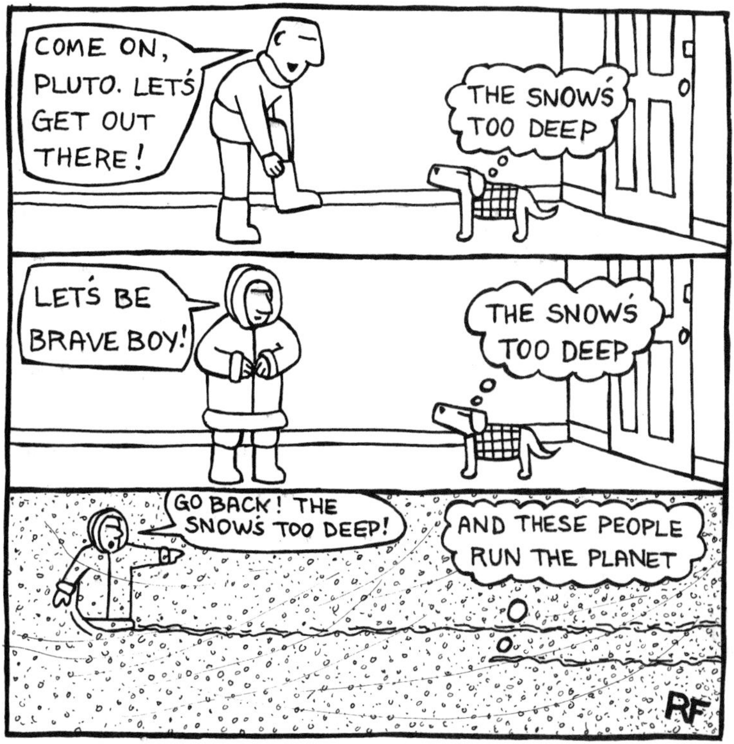
COME ON, PLUTO. LET'S GET OUT THERE!
THE SNOW'S TOO DEEP
LET'S BE BRAVE BOY!
THE SNOW'S TOO DEEP
GO BACK! THE SNOW'S TOO DEEP!
AND THESE PEOPLE RUN THE PLANET
RF

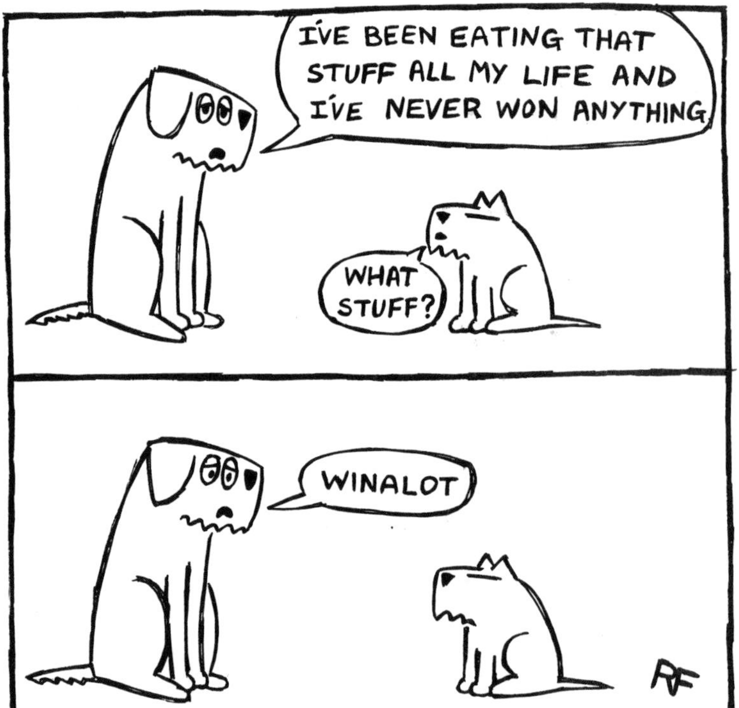
I'VE BEEN EATING THAT STUFF ALL MY LIFE AND I'VE NEVER WON ANYTHING
WHAT STUFF?
WINALOT
RF

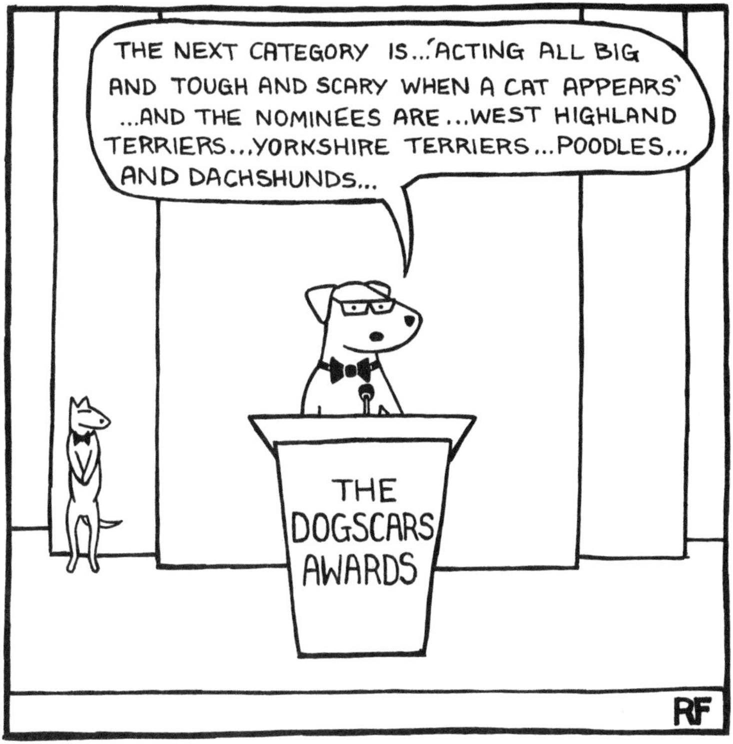
THE NEXT CATEGORY IS...'ACTING ALL BIG AND TOUGH AND SCARY WHEN A CAT APPEARS' ...AND THE NOMINEES ARE...WEST HIGHLAND TERRIERS...YORKSHIRE TERRIERS...POODLES... AND DACHSHUNDS...
THE DOGSCARS AWARDS
RF

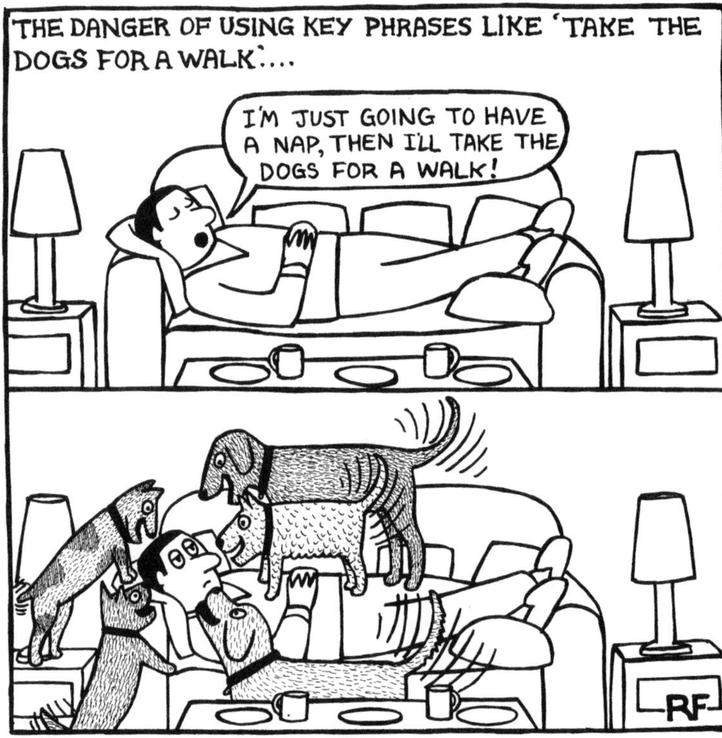
THE DANGER OF USING KEY PHRASES LIKE 'TAKE THE DOGS FOR A WALK'....
I'M JUST GOING TO HAVE A NAP, THEN I'LL TAKE THE DOGS FOR A WALK!
RF

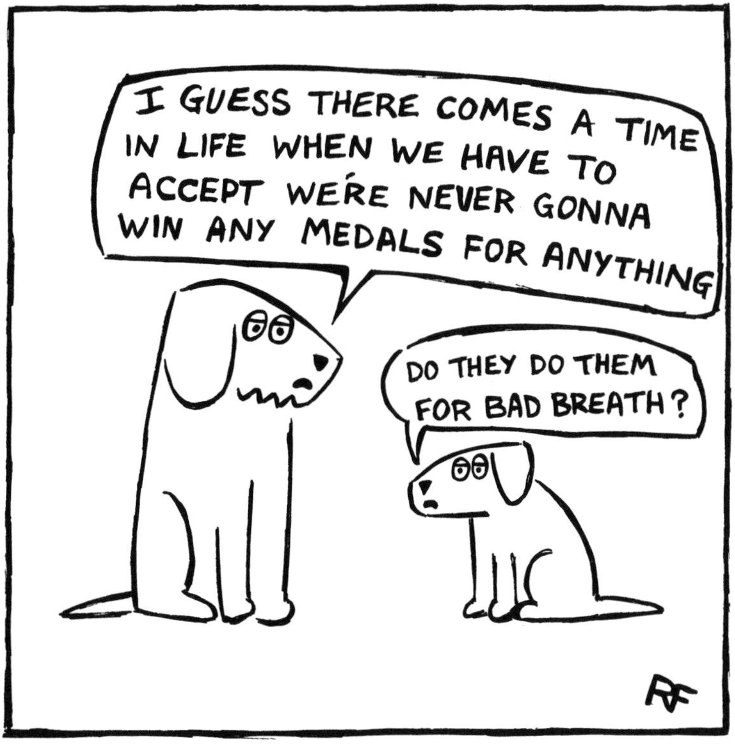
I GUESS THERE COMES A TIME IN LIFE WHEN WE HAVE TO ACCEPT WE'RE NEVER GONNA WIN ANY MEDALS FOR ANYTHING
DO THEY DO THEM FOR BAD BREATH?
RF

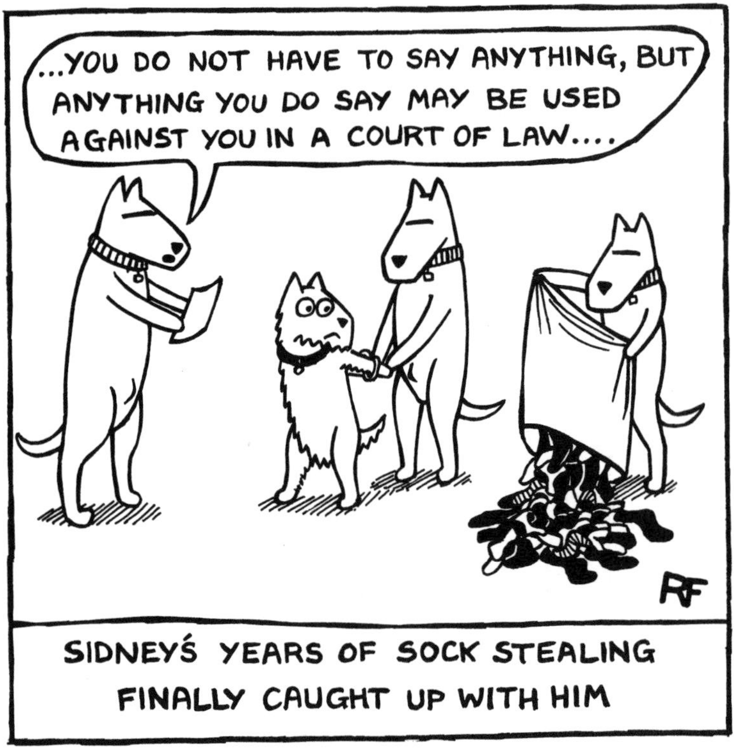
...YOU DO NOT HAVE TO SAY ANYTHING, BUT ANYTHING YOU DO SAY MAY BE USED AGAINST YOU IN A COURT OF LAW....
RF

SIDNEY'S YEARS OF SOCK STEALING FINALLY CAUGHT UP WITH HIM

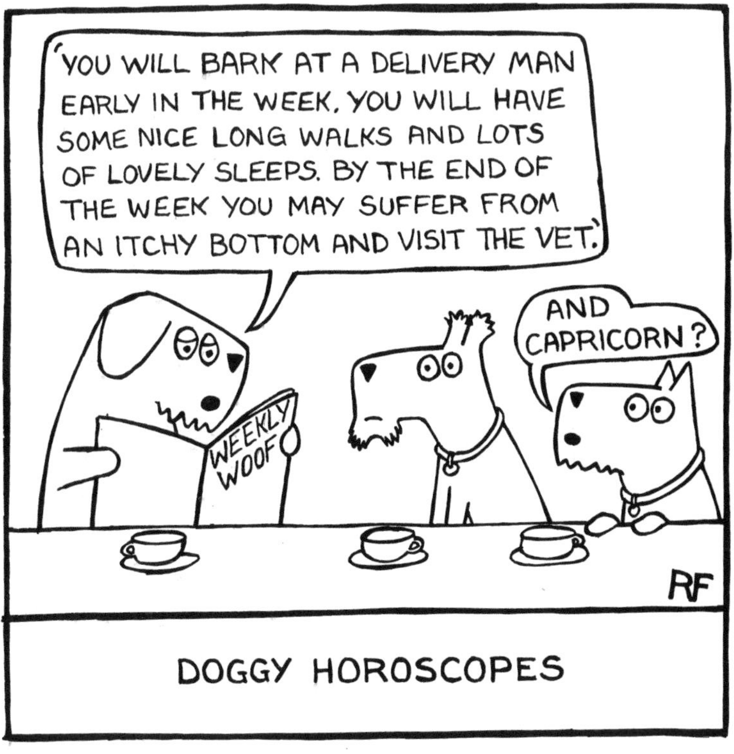
'YOU WILL BARK AT A DELIVERY MAN EARLY IN THE WEEK. YOU WILL HAVE SOME NICE LONG WALKS AND LOTS OF LOVELY SLEEPS. BY THE END OF THE WEEK YOU MAY SUFFER FROM AN ITCHY BOTTOM AND VISIT THE VET.'
WEEKLY WOOF
AND CAPRICORN?
RF

DOGGY HOROSCOPES

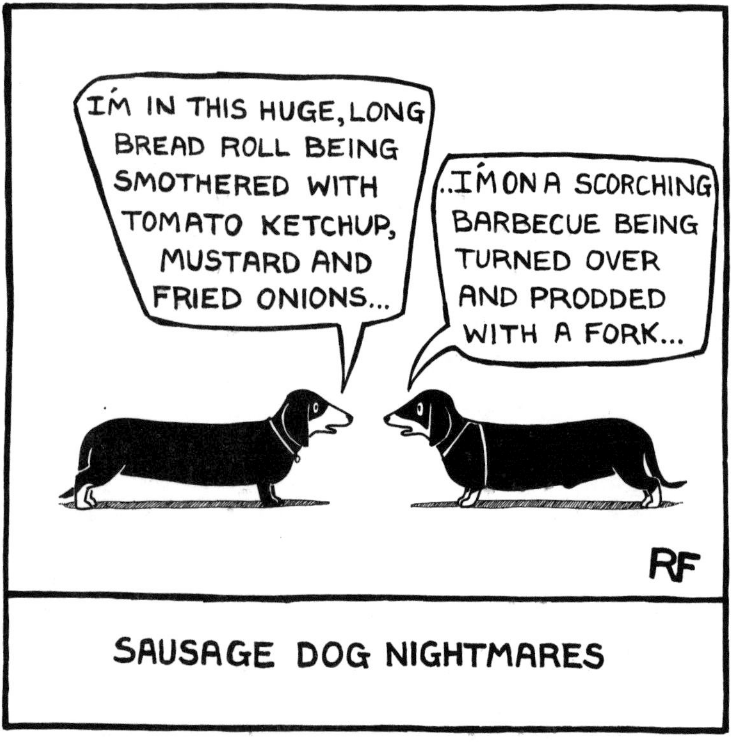
I'M IN THIS HUGE, LONG BREAD ROLL BEING SMOTHERED WITH TOMATO KETCHUP, MUSTARD AND FRIED ONIONS...
..I'M ON A SCORCHING BARBECUE BEING TURNED OVER AND PRODDED WITH A FORK...
RF

SAUSAGE DOG NIGHTMARES

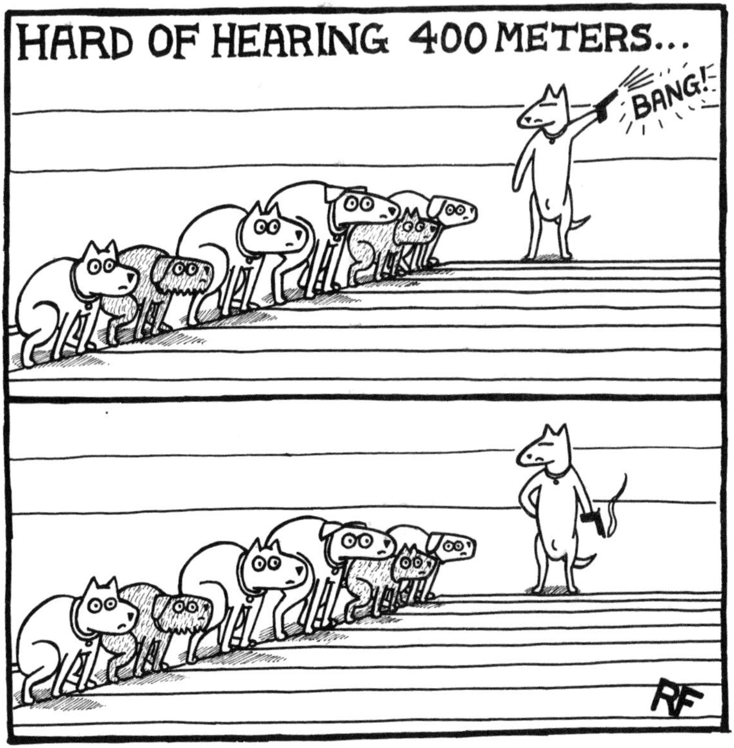
HARD OF HEARING 400 METERS...
BANG!
RF

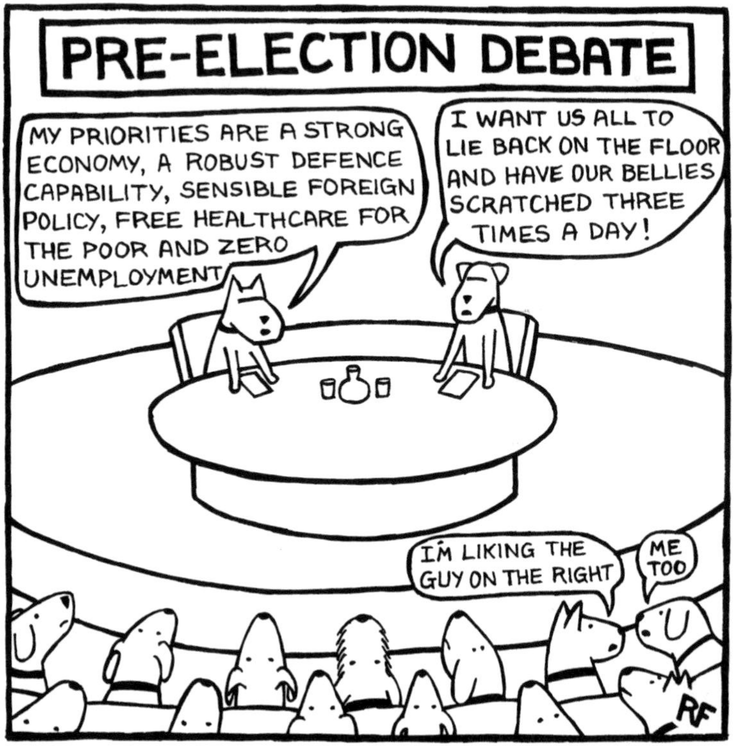
PRE-ELECTION DEBATE
MY PRIORITIES ARE A STRONG ECONOMY, A ROBUST DEFENCE CAPABILITY, SENSIBLE FOREIGN POLICY, FREE HEALTHCARE FOR THE POOR AND ZERO UNEMPLOYMENT
I WANT US ALL TO LIE BACK ON THE FLOOR AND HAVE OUR BELLIES SCRATCHED THREE TIMES A DAY!
I'M LIKING THE GUY ON THE RIGHT
ME TOO
RF

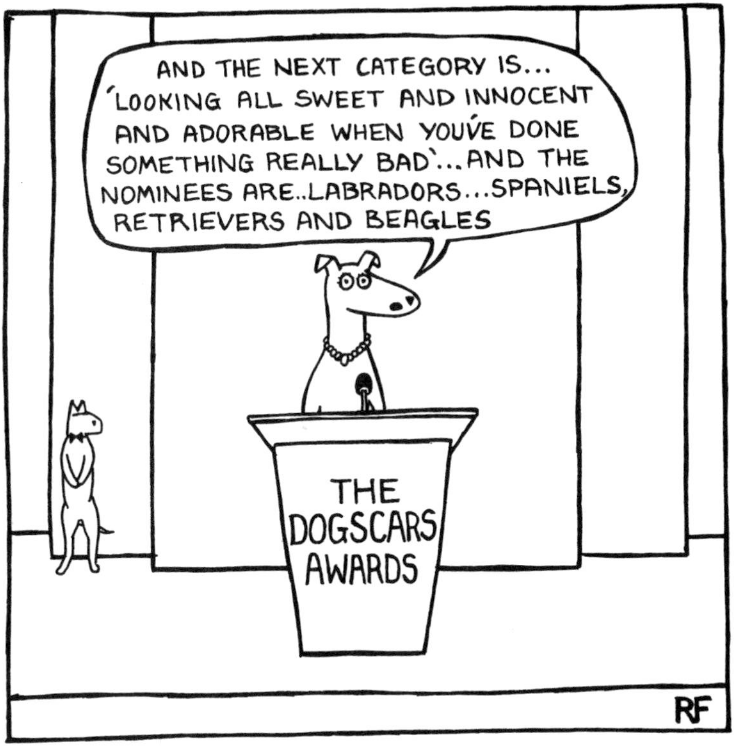
AND THE NEXT CATEGORY IS... 'LOOKING ALL SWEET AND INNOCENT AND ADORABLE WHEN YOU'VE DONE SOMETHING REALLY BAD'... AND THE NOMINEES ARE..LABRADORS...SPANIELS, RETRIEVERS AND BEAGLES
THE DOGSCARS AWARDS
RF

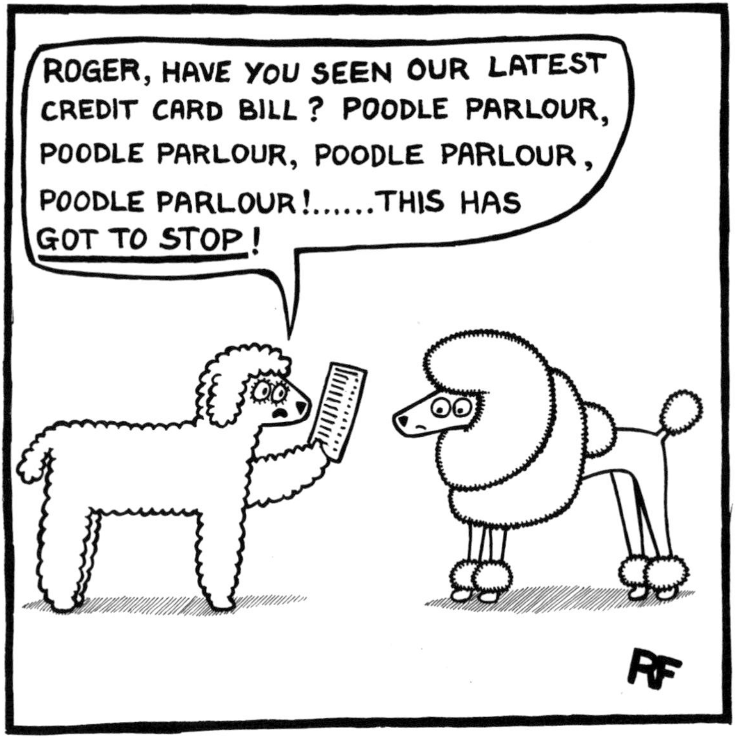
ROGER, HAVE YOU SEEN OUR LATEST CREDIT CARD BILL ? POODLE PARLOUR, POODLE PARLOUR, POODLE PARLOUR, POODLE PARLOUR!......THIS HAS GOT TO STOP!
RF

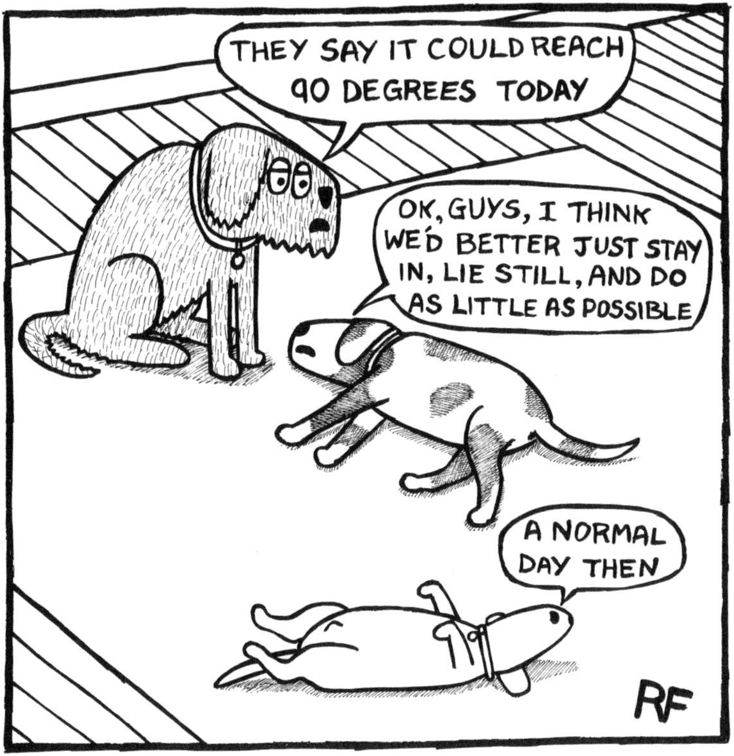
THEY SAY IT COULD REACH 90 DEGREES TODAY
OK, GUYS, I THINK WE'D BETTER JUST STAY IN, LIE STILL, AND DO AS LITTLE AS POSSIBLE
A NORMAL DAY THEN
RF

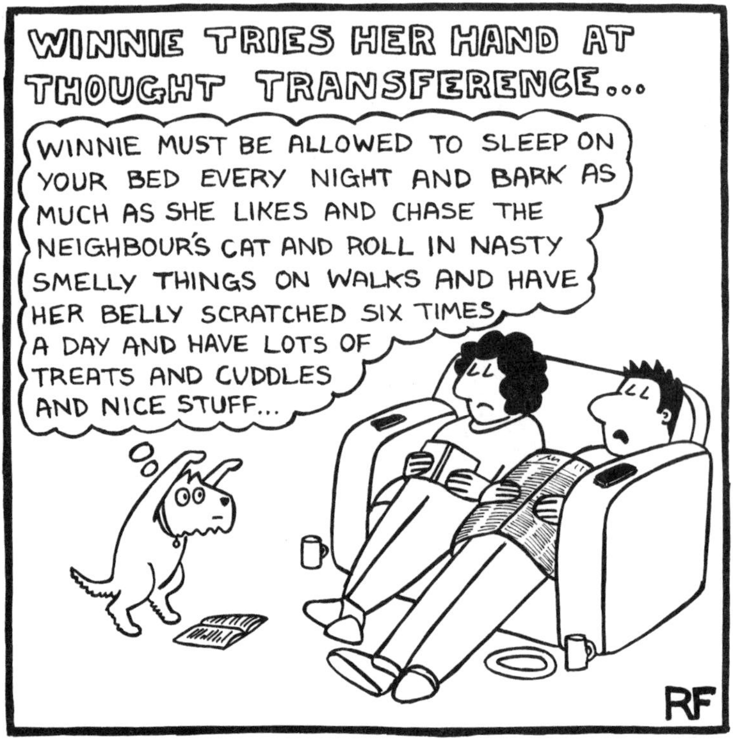
WINNIE TRIES HER HAND AT THOUGHT TRANSFERENCE...
WINNIE MUST BE ALLOWED TO SLEEP ON YOUR BED EVERY NIGHT AND BARK AS MUCH AS SHE LIKES AND CHASE THE NEIGHBOUR'S CAT AND ROLL IN NASTY SMELLY THINGS ON WALKS AND HAVE HER BELLY SCRATCHED SIX TIMES A DAY AND HAVE LOTS OF TREATS AND CUDDLES AND NICE STUFF...
RF

BOB AND SUE LIKED NOTHING MORE THAN
A QUIET EVENING IN FRONT OF
THE TV WITH THE DOGS

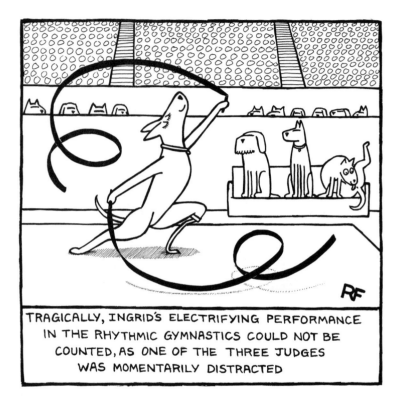

TRAGICALLY, INGRID'S ELECTRIFYING PERFORMANCE
IN THE RHYTHMIC GYMNASTICS COULD NOT BE
COUNTED, AS ONE OF THE THREE JUDGES
WAS MOMENTARILY DISTRACTED

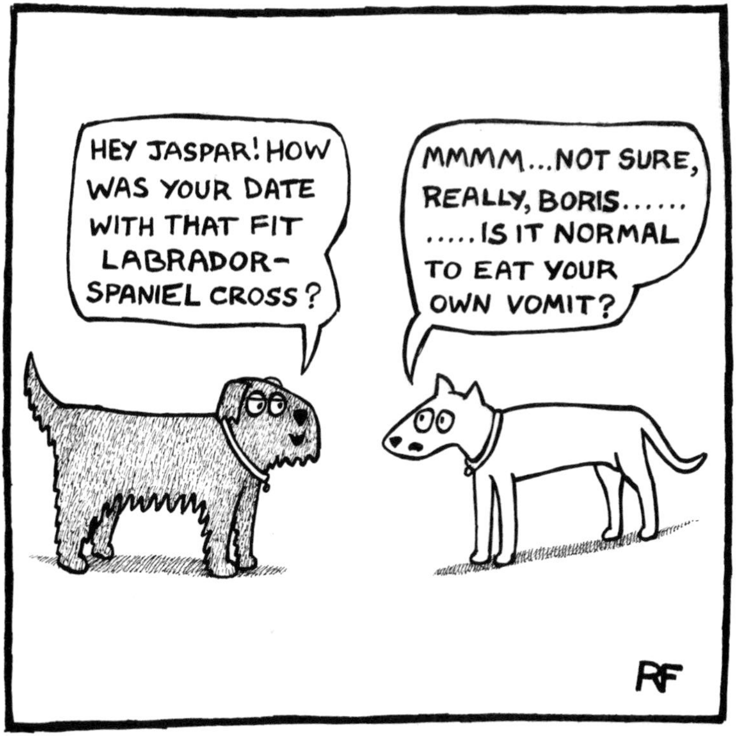
HEY JASPAR! HOW WAS YOUR DATE WITH THAT FIT LABRADOR-SPANIEL CROSS?
MMMM...NOT SURE, REALLY, BORIS...... .....IS IT NORMAL TO EAT YOUR OWN VOMIT?
RF

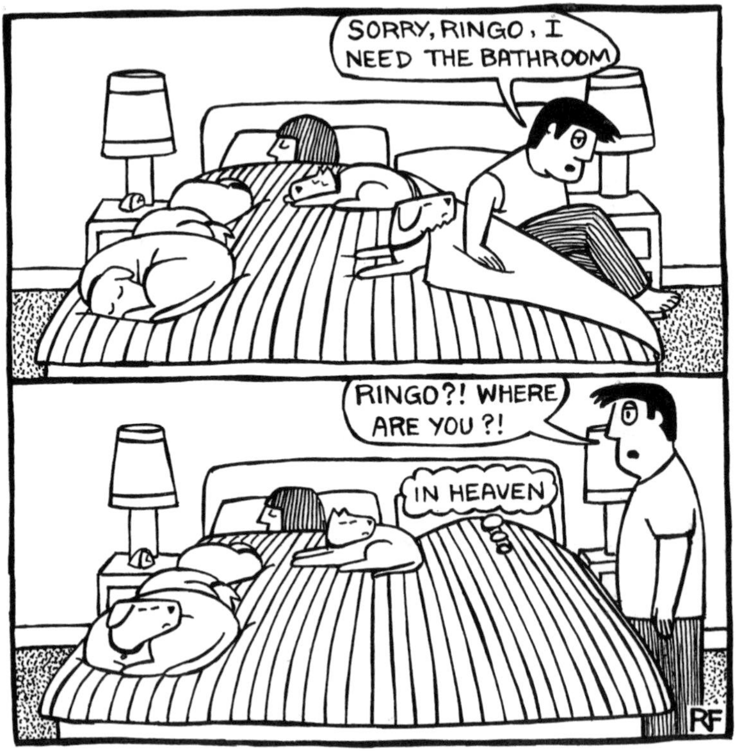
SORRY, RINGO, I NEED THE BATHROOM
RINGO?! WHERE ARE YOU?!
IN HEAVEN
RF

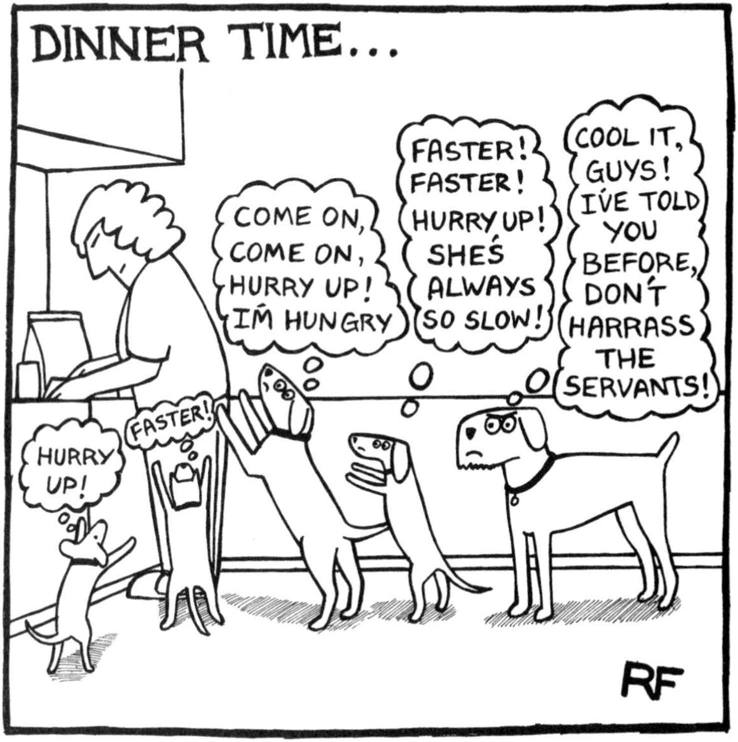
DINNER TIME...
HURRY UP!
FASTER!
COME ON, COME ON, HURRY UP! I'M HUNGRY
FASTER! FASTER! HURRY UP! SHE'S ALWAYS SO SLOW!
COOL IT, GUYS! I'VE TOLD YOU BEFORE, DON'T HARRASS THE SERVANTS!
RF

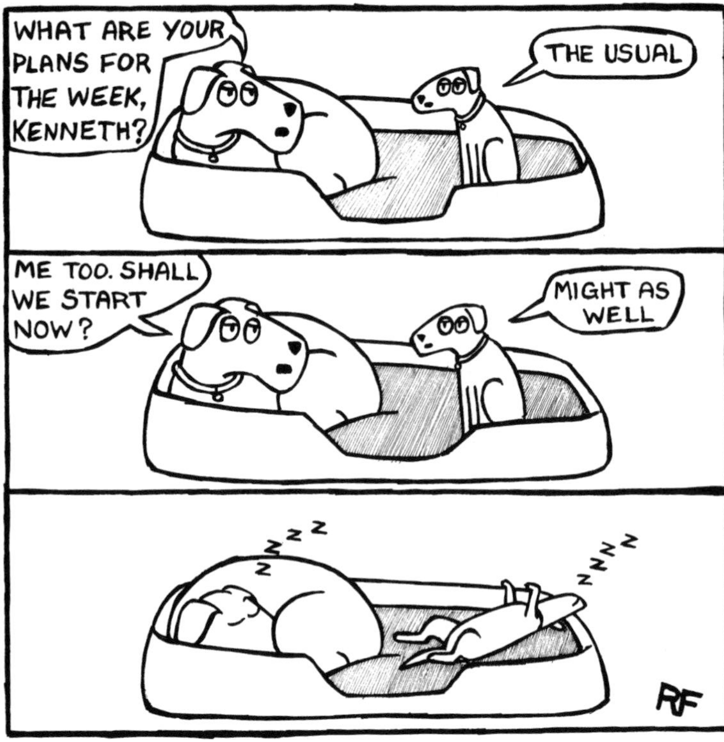
WHAT ARE YOUR PLANS FOR THE WEEK, KENNETH?
THE USUAL
ME TOO. SHALL WE START NOW?
MIGHT AS WELL
ZZZZ
ZZZZ
RF

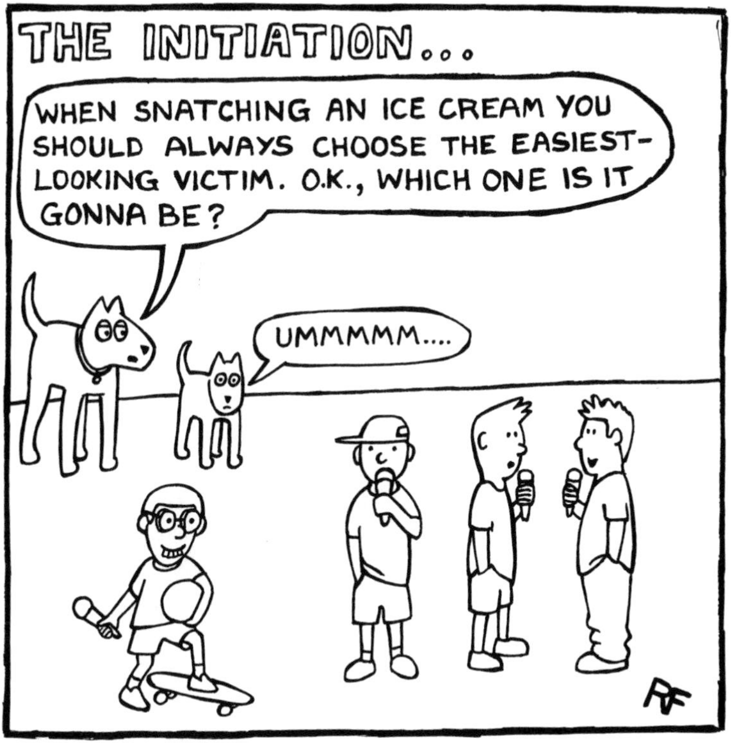
THE INITIATION...
WHEN SNATCHING AN ICE CREAM YOU SHOULD ALWAYS CHOOSE THE EASIEST-LOOKING VICTIM. O.K., WHICH ONE IS IT GONNA BE?
UMMMMM....
RF

PIDDLE!
PUDDLE!
WRIGGLE!
CUDDLE!
RF

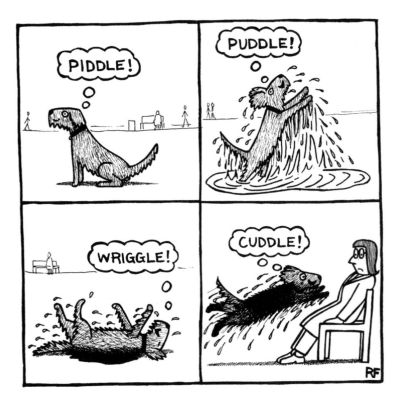

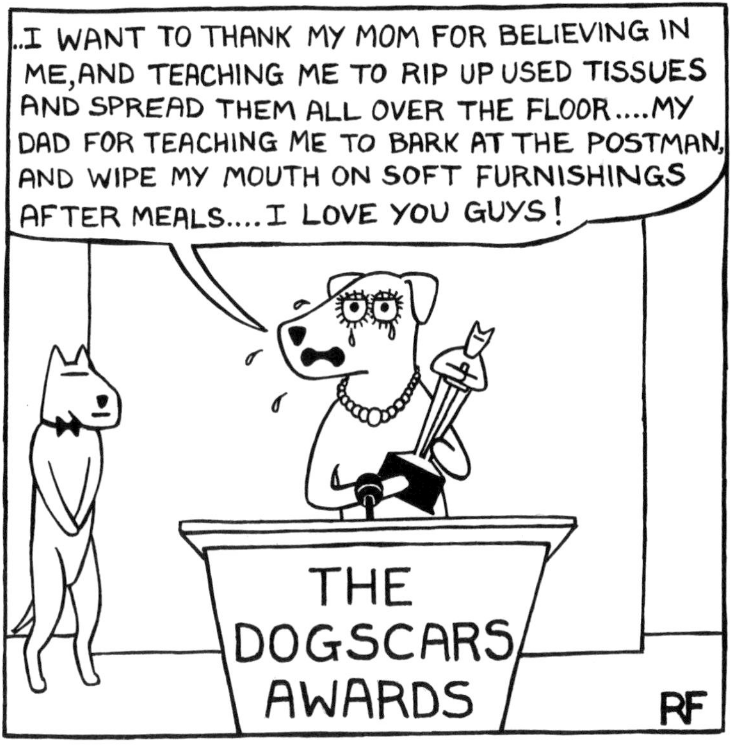
..I WANT TO THANK MY MOM FOR BELIEVING IN ME, AND TEACHING ME TO RIP UP USED TISSUES AND SPREAD THEM ALL OVER THE FLOOR....MY DAD FOR TEACHING ME TO BARK AT THE POSTMAN, AND WIPE MY MOUTH ON SOFT FURNISHINGS AFTER MEALS....I LOVE YOU GUYS!
THE DOGSCARS AWARDS
RF

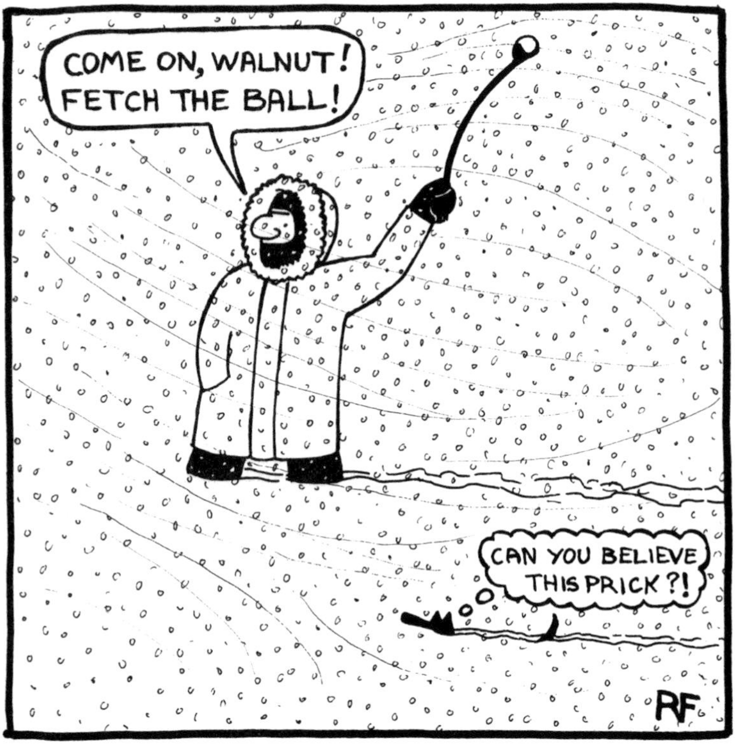
COME ON, WALNUT! FETCH THE BALL!
CAN YOU BELIEVE THIS PRICK?!
RF

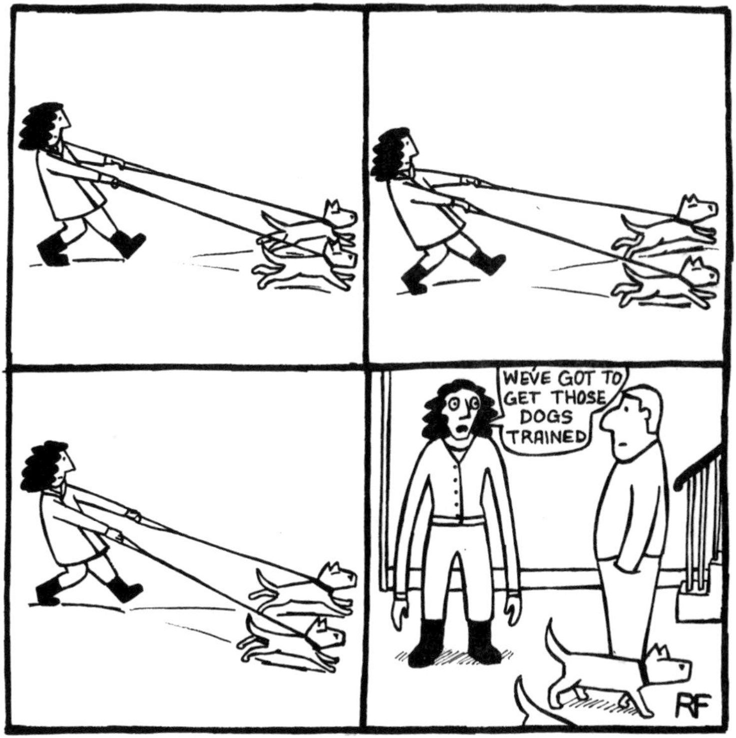
WE'VE GOT TO GET THOSE DOGS TRAINED
RF

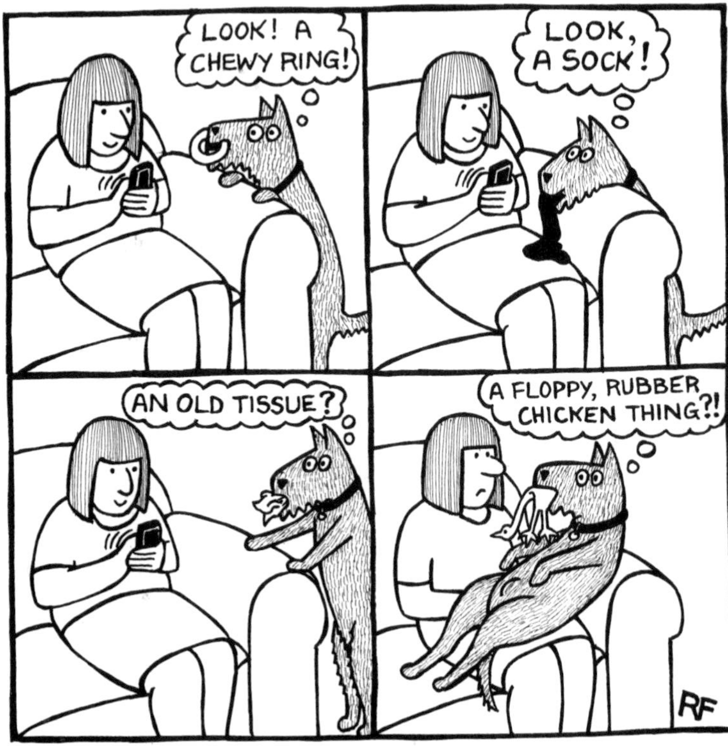
LOOK! A CHEWY RING!
LOOK, A SOCK!
AN OLD TISSUE?
A FLOPPY, RUBBER CHICKEN THING?!
RF

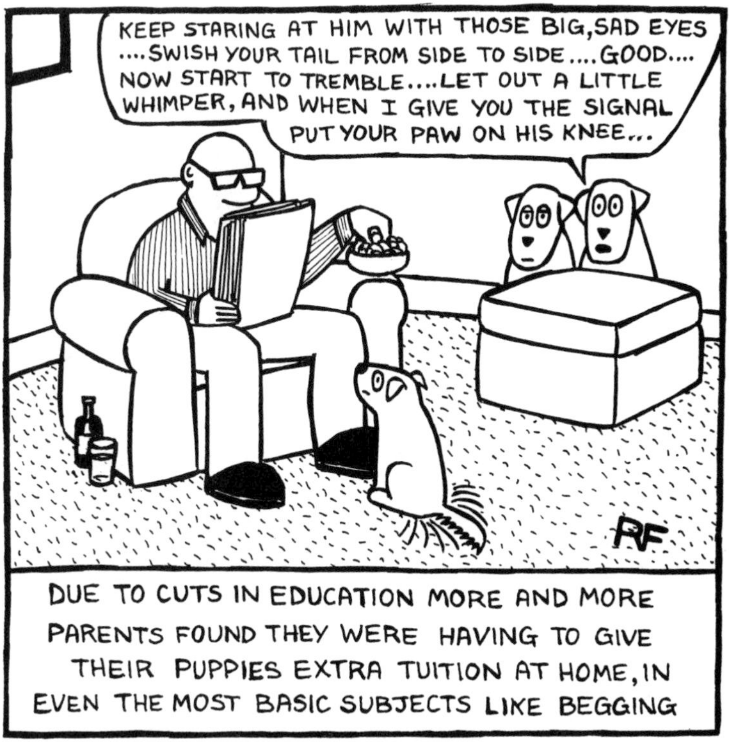
KEEP STARING AT HIM WITH THOSE BIG, SAD EYES ....SWISH YOUR TAIL FROM SIDE TO SIDE....GOOD.... NOW START TO TREMBLE....LET OUT A LITTLE WHIMPER, AND WHEN I GIVE YOU THE SIGNAL PUT YOUR PAW ON HIS KNEE...
RF
DUE TO CUTS IN EDUCATION MORE AND MORE PARENTS FOUND THEY WERE HAVING TO GIVE THEIR PUPPIES EXTRA TUITION AT HOME, IN EVEN THE MOST BASIC SUBJECTS LIKE BEGGING

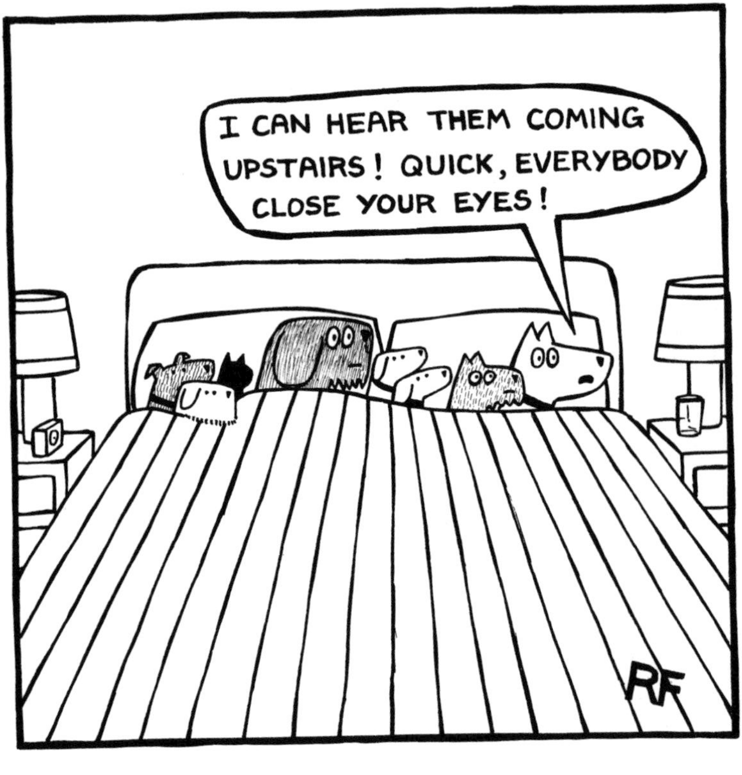
I CAN HEAR THEM COMING UPSTAIRS! QUICK, EVERYBODY CLOSE YOUR EYES!
RF

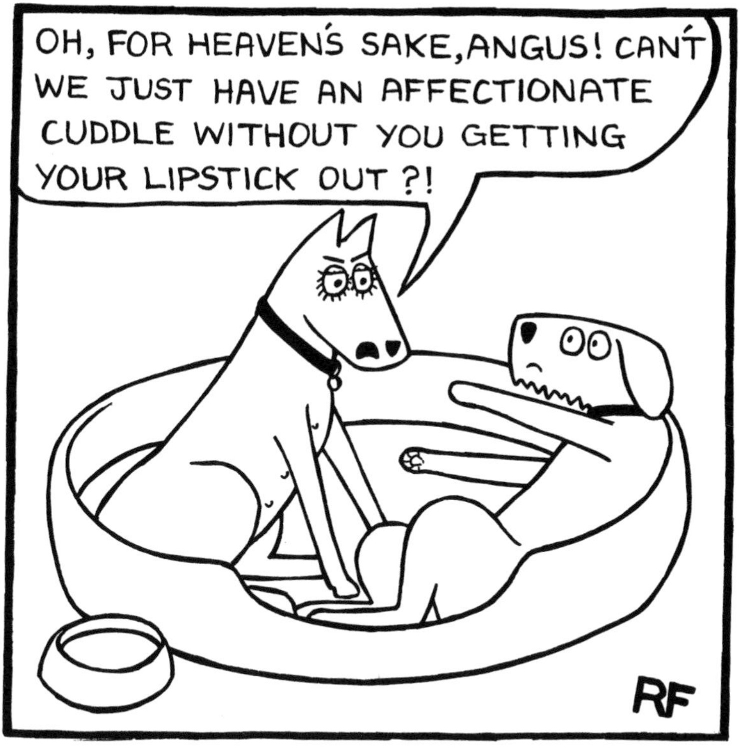
OH, FOR HEAVEN'S SAKE, ANGUS! CAN'T WE JUST HAVE AN AFFECTIONATE CUDDLE WITHOUT YOU GETTING YOUR LIPSTICK OUT ?!
RF

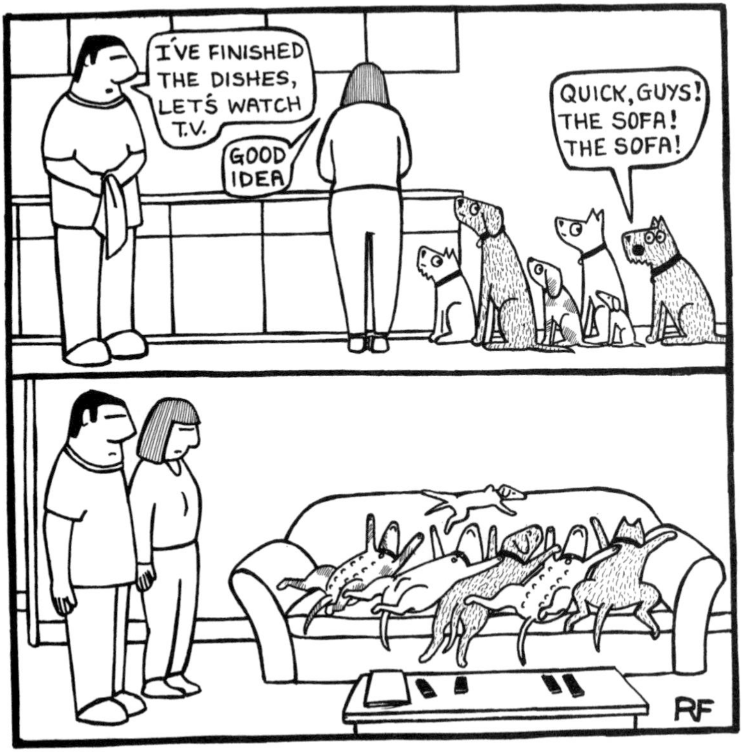
I'VE FINISHED THE DISHES, LET'S WATCH T.V.
GOOD IDEA
QUICK, GUYS! THE SOFA! THE SOFA!
RF

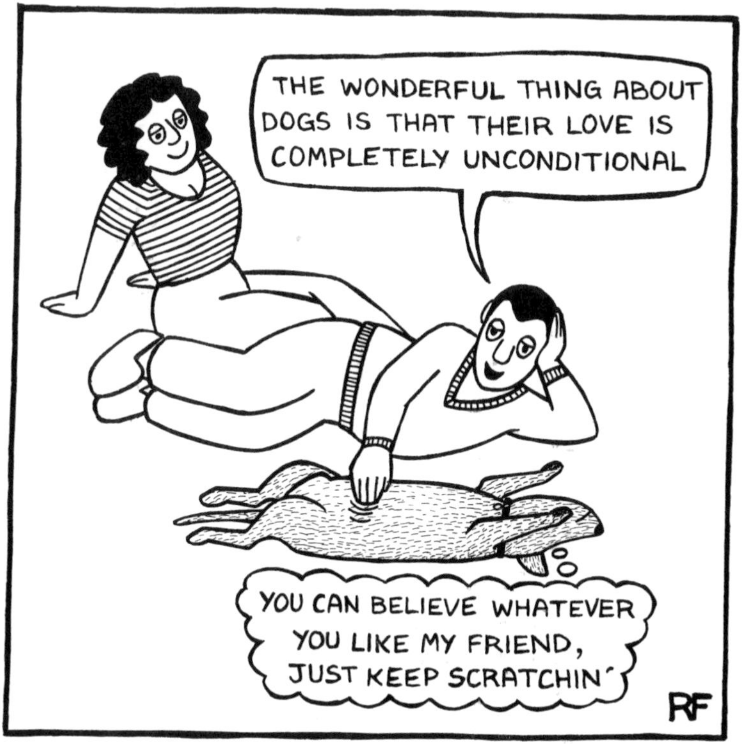
THE WONDERFUL THING ABOUT DOGS IS THAT THEIR LOVE IS COMPLETELY UNCONDITIONAL
YOU CAN BELIEVE WHATEVER YOU LIKE MY FRIEND, JUST KEEP SCRATCHIN'
RF

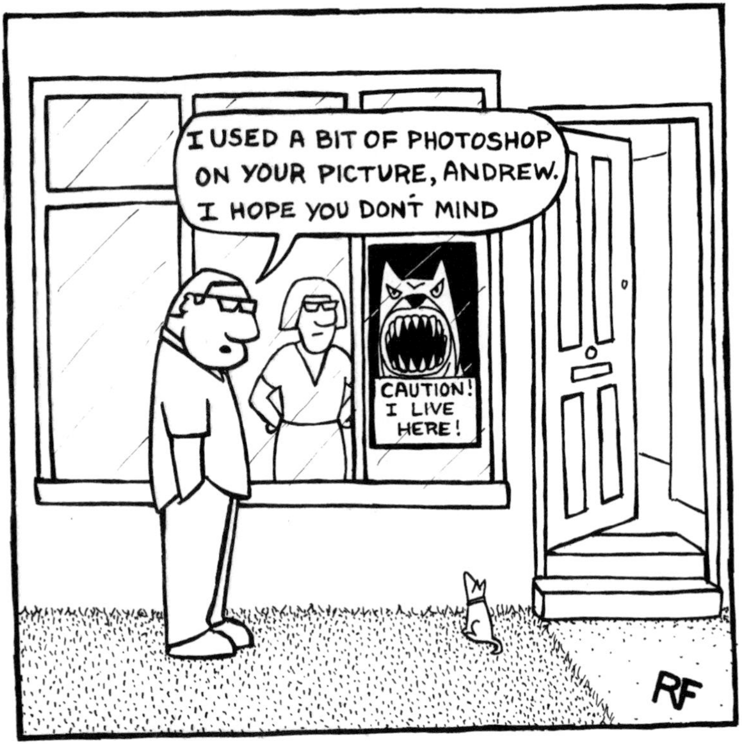
I USED A BIT OF PHOTOSHOP ON YOUR PICTURE, ANDREW. I HOPE YOU DON'T MIND
CAUTION! I LIVE HERE!
RF

COUPLES THERAPY....
DO YOU REALISE HOW EMBARRASSING IT IS WHEN WE GO OUT FOR A WALK AND YOU KEEP STOPPING AND DRINKING FROM MUDDY PUDDLES?
ISSUES
TISSUES
RF

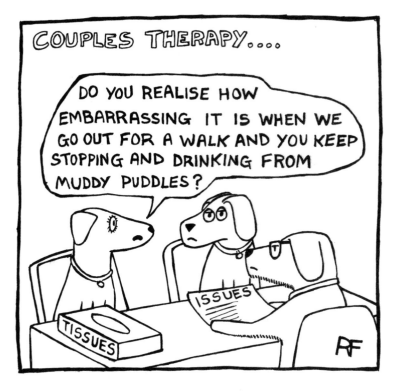

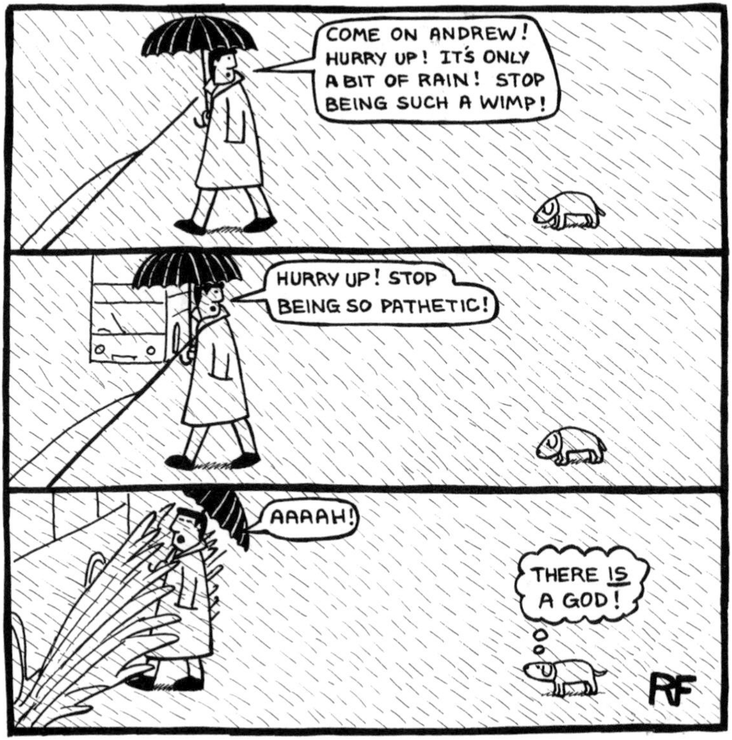
COME ON ANDREW! HURRY UP! IT'S ONLY A BIT OF RAIN! STOP BEING SUCH A WIMP!
HURRY UP! STOP BEING SO PATHETIC!
AAAAH!
THERE IS A GOD!
RF

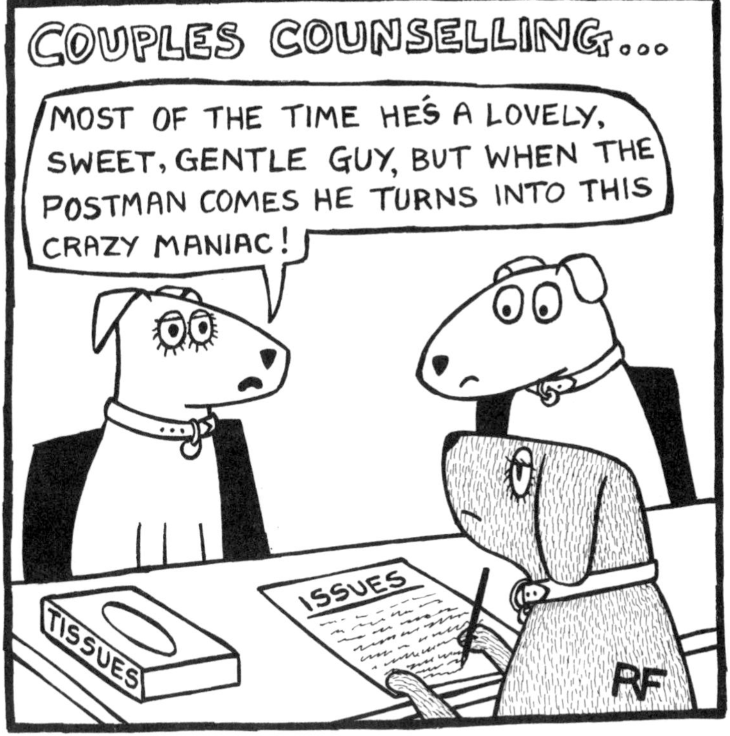
COUPLES COUNSELLING...
MOST OF THE TIME HE'S A LOVELY, SWEET, GENTLE GUY, BUT WHEN THE POSTMAN COMES HE TURNS INTO THIS CRAZY MANIAC!
ISSUES
TISSUES
RF

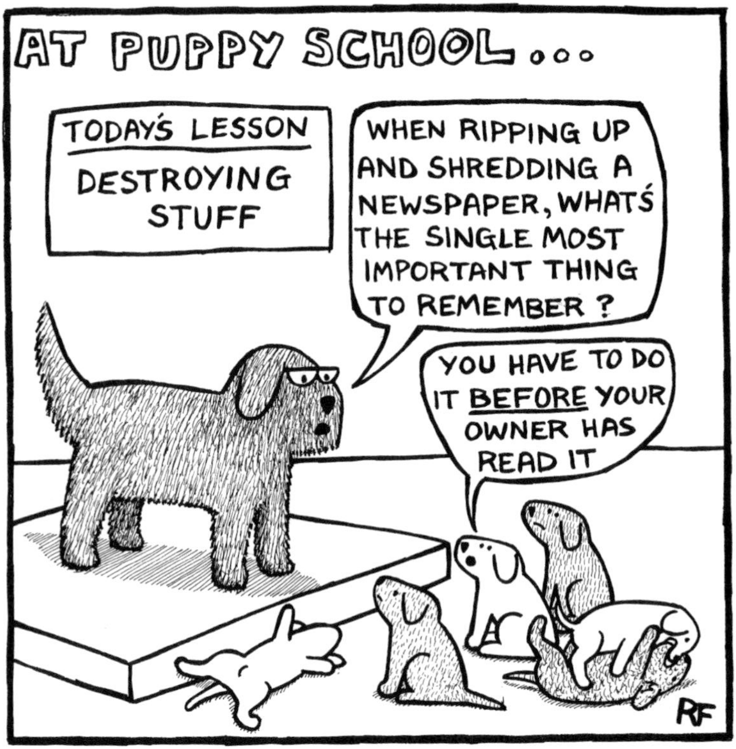
AT PUPPY SCHOOL...
TODAY'S LESSON
DESTROYING STUFF
WHEN RIPPING UP AND SHREDDING A NEWSPAPER, WHAT'S THE SINGLE MOST IMPORTANT THING TO REMEMBER?
YOU HAVE TO DO IT BEFORE YOUR OWNER HAS READ IT
RF

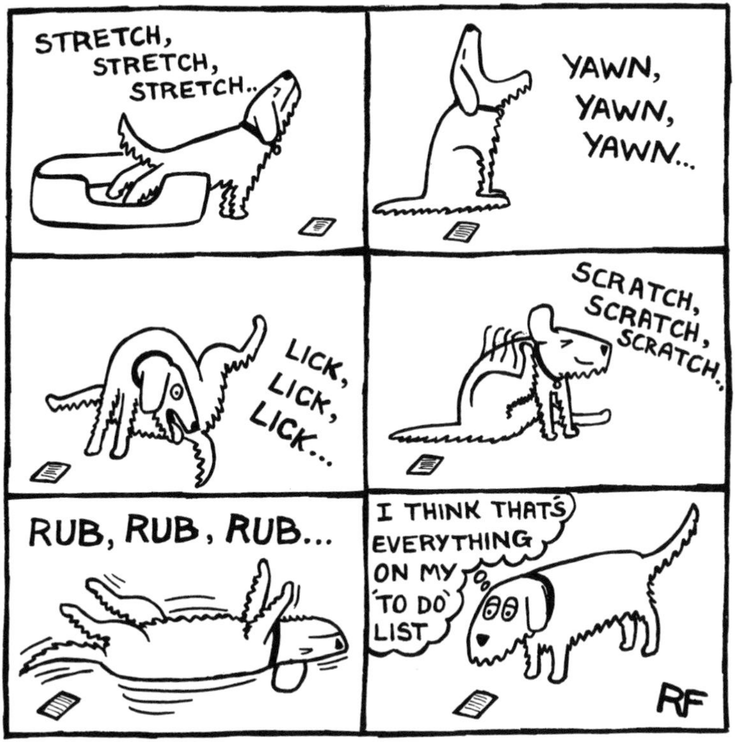
STRETCH,
STRETCH,
STRETCH..
YAWN,
YAWN,
YAWN...
LICK,
LICK,
LICK...
SCRATCH,
SCRATCH,
SCRATCH..
RUB, RUB, RUB...
I THINK THAT'S EVERYTHING ON MY 'TO DO' LIST
RF

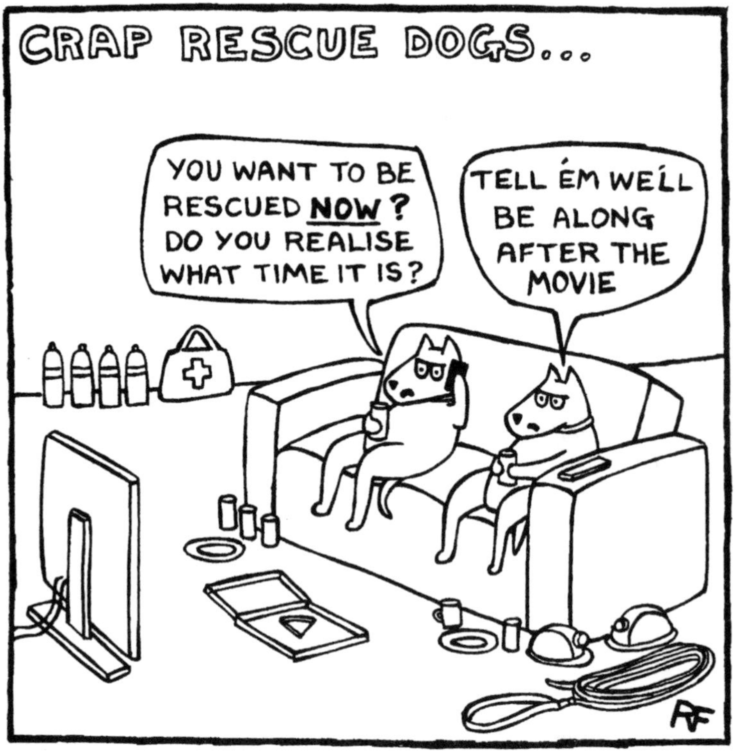
CRAP RESCUE DOGS...
YOU WANT TO BE RESCUED NOW? DO YOU REALISE WHAT TIME IT IS?
TELL ÉM WEĹL BE ALONG AFTER THE MOVIE
RF

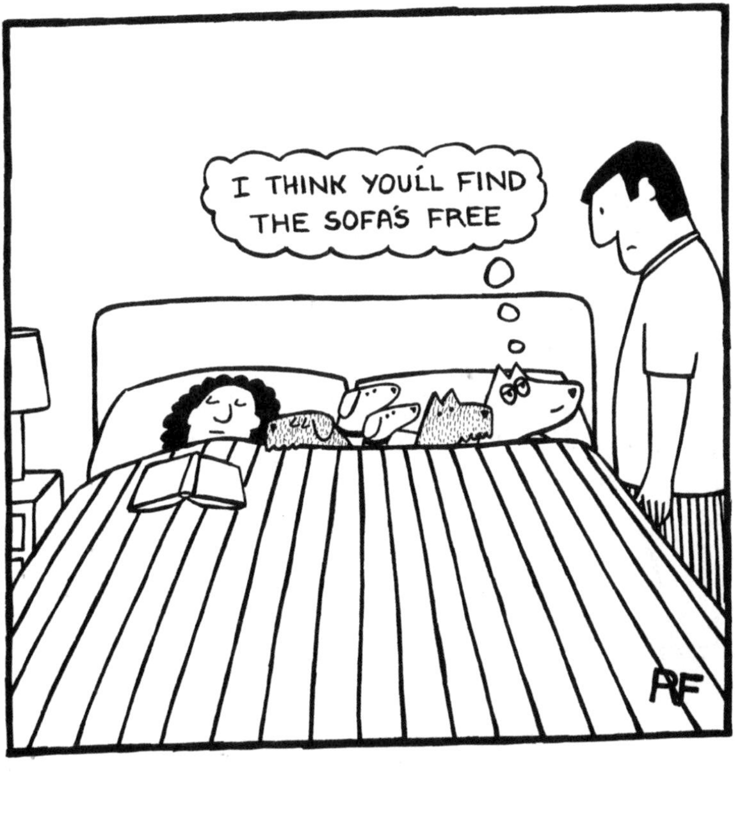
I THINK YOU'LL FIND THE SOFA'S FREE
RF

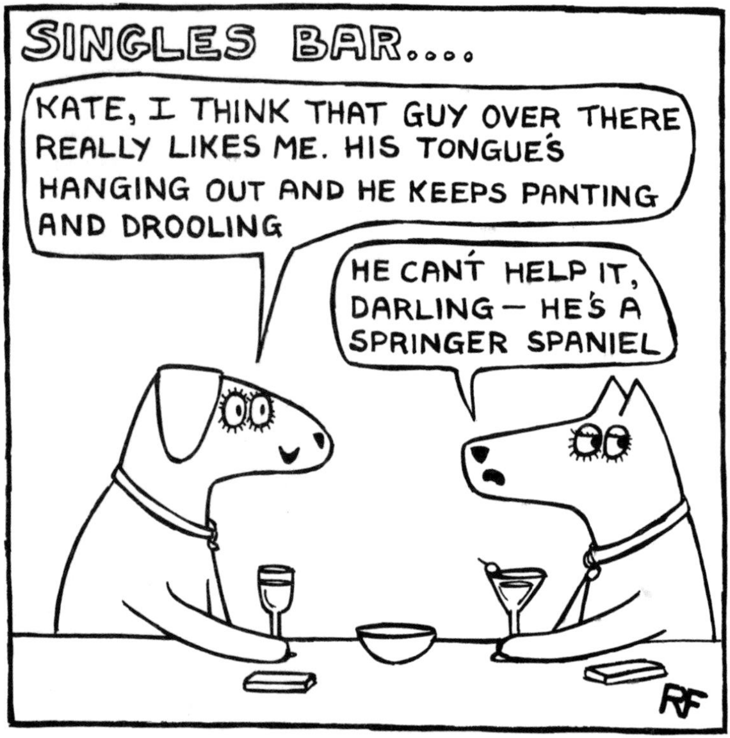
SINGLES BAR....
KATE, I THINK THAT GUY OVER THERE REALLY LIKES ME. HIS TONGUE'S HANGING OUT AND HE KEEPS PANTING AND DROOLING
HE CAN'T HELP IT, DARLING — HE'S A SPRINGER SPANIEL
RF

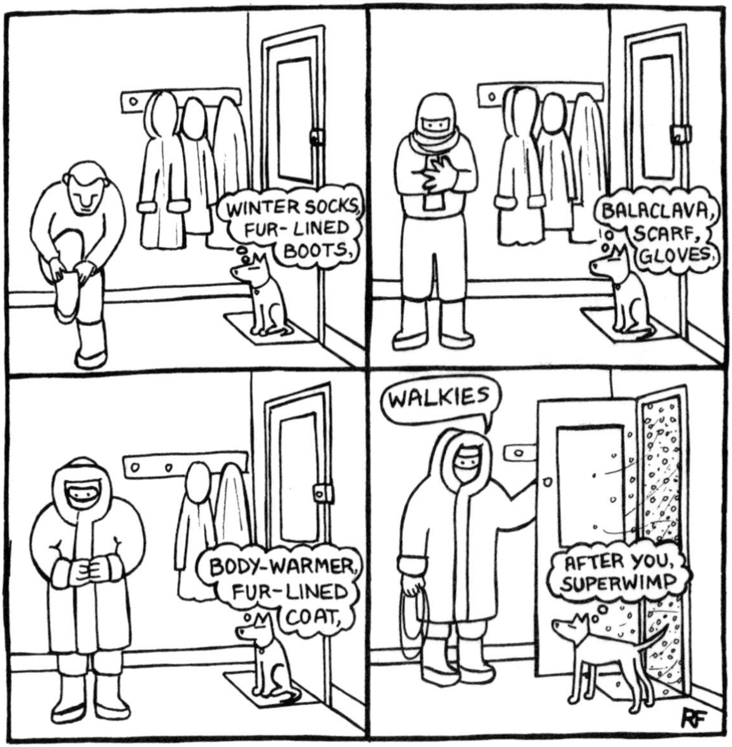
WINTER SOCKS, FUR-LINED BOOTS,
BALACLAVA, SCARF, GLOVES,
BODY-WARMER, FUR-LINED COAT,
WALKIES
AFTER YOU, SUPERWIMP
RF

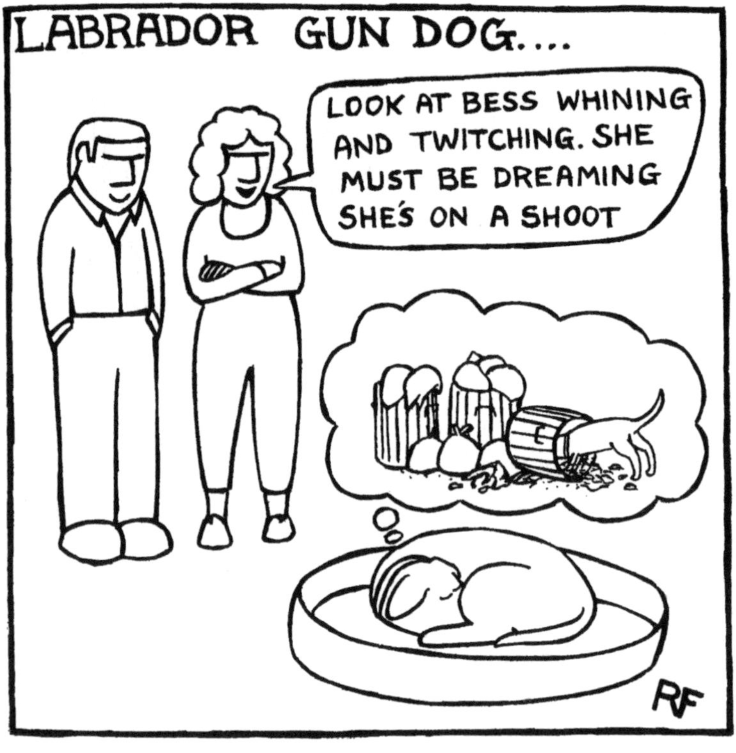
LABRADOR GUN DOG....
LOOK AT BESS WHINING AND TWITCHING. SHE MUST BE DREAMING SHE'S ON A SHOOT
RF

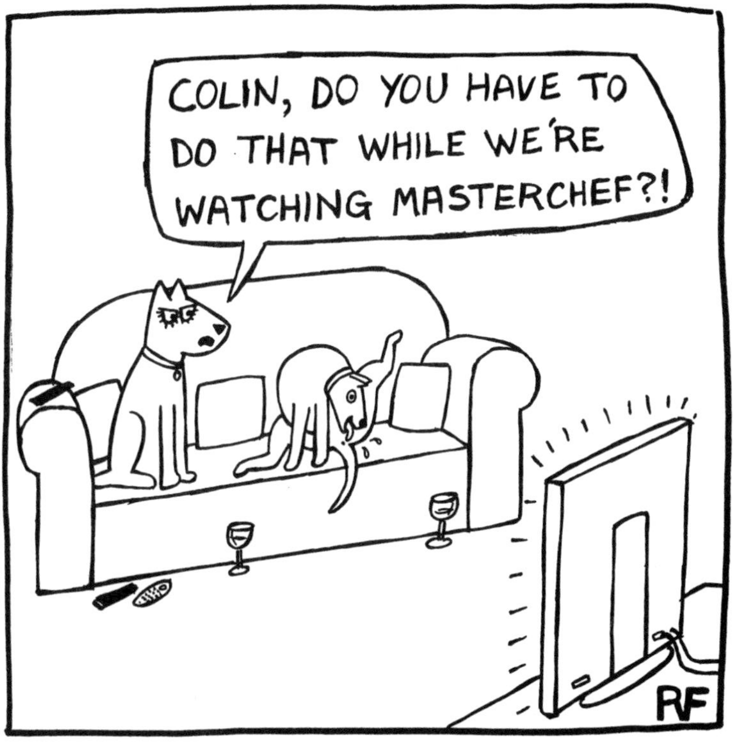
COLIN, DO YOU HAVE TO DO THAT WHILE WE'RE WATCHING MASTERCHEF?!
RF

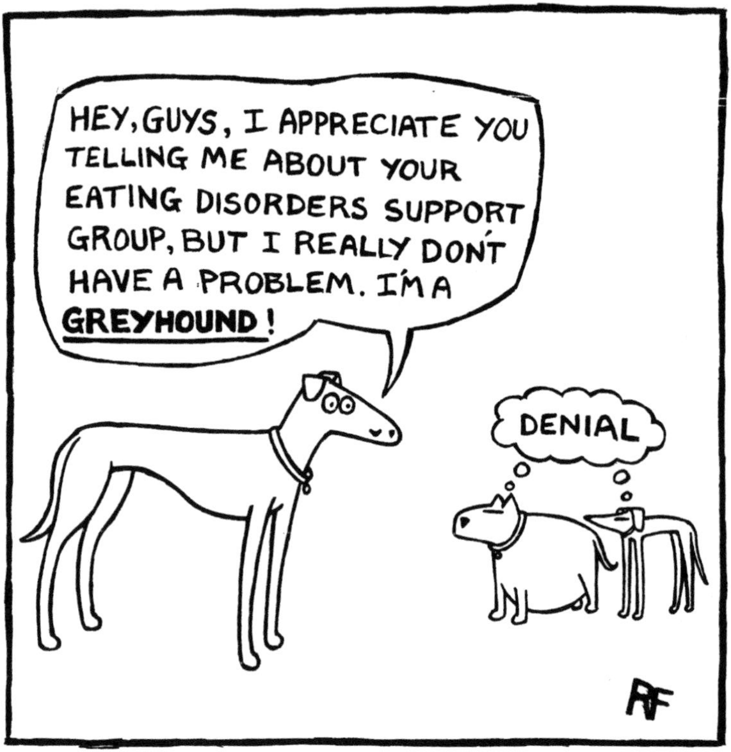
HEY, GUYS, I APPRECIATE YOU TELLING ME ABOUT YOUR EATING DISORDERS SUPPORT GROUP, BUT I REALLY DON'T HAVE A PROBLEM. I'M A **GREYHOUND**!
DENIAL
RF

PUPPY EDUCATION...
UNDER HIS BUTT IS 'THE WARM SPOT', A VERY, VERY SPECIAL PLACE, AND IT'S A DOG'S JOB TO TAKE IT. BE PATIENT AND EVENTUALLY HE'LL NEED THE BATHROOM, THEN YOU POUNCE!
NEWS
AND WHEN HE RETURNS FROM THE BATHROOM?
PRETEND YOU ARE DEEPLY ASLEEP, AND IF HE TRIES TO MOVE YOU, GROWL!
NEWS
RF

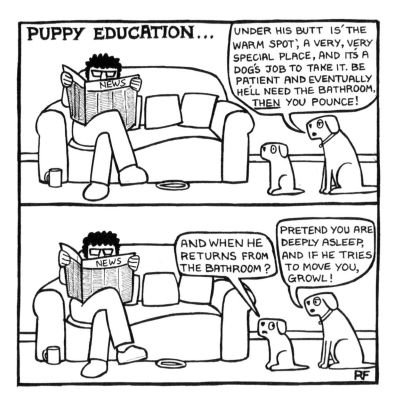

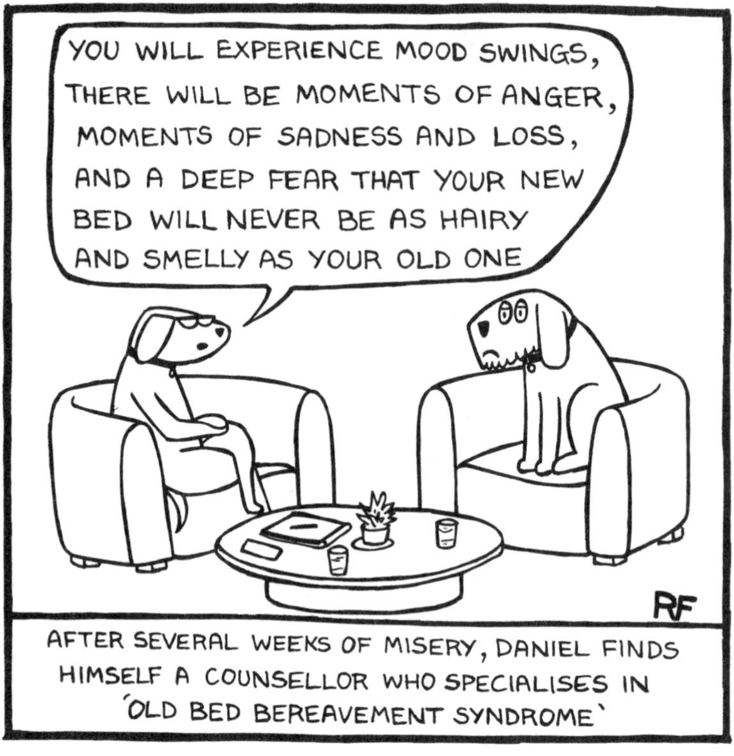
YOU WILL EXPERIENCE MOOD SWINGS, THERE WILL BE MOMENTS OF ANGER, MOMENTS OF SADNESS AND LOSS, AND A DEEP FEAR THAT YOUR NEW BED WILL NEVER BE AS HAIRY AND SMELLY AS YOUR OLD ONE
RF

AFTER SEVERAL WEEKS OF MISERY, DANIEL FINDS HIMSELF A COUNSELLOR WHO SPECIALISES IN 'OLD BED BEREAVEMENT SYNDROME'

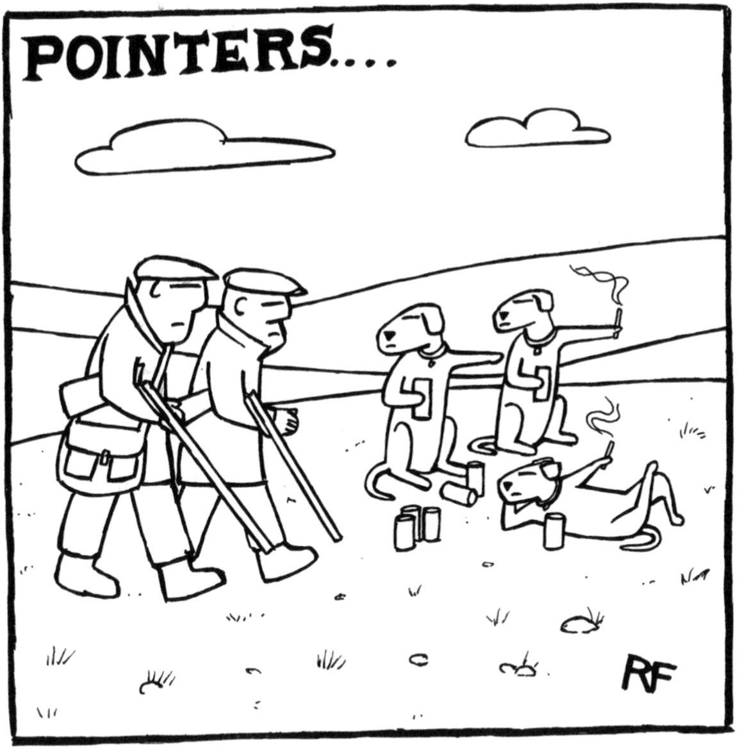
POINTERS....
RF

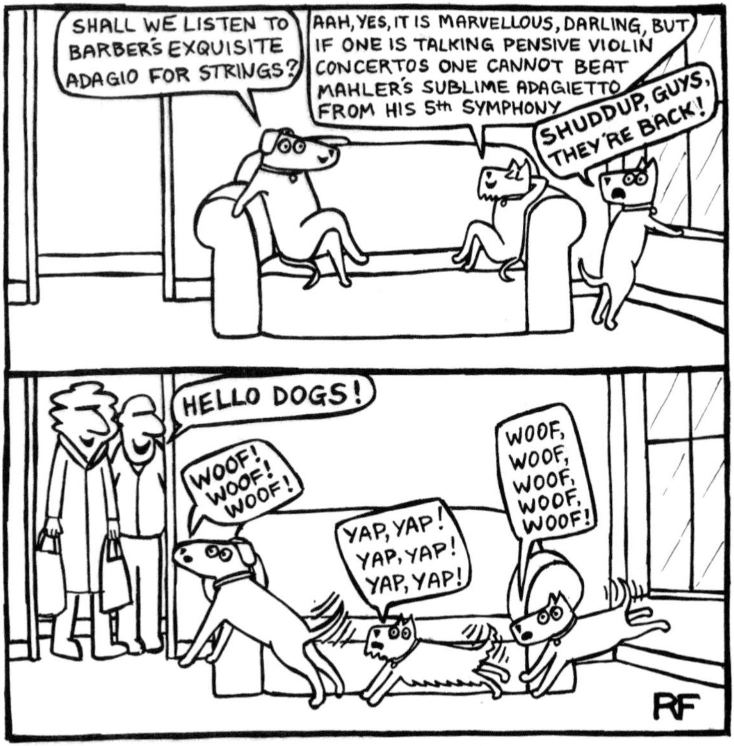
SHALL WE LISTEN TO BARBER'S EXQUISITE ADAGIO FOR STRINGS?
AAH, YES, IT IS MARVELLOUS, DARLING, BUT IF ONE IS TALKING PENSIVE VIOLIN CONCERTOS ONE CANNOT BEAT MAHLER'S SUBLIME ADAGIETTO FROM HIS 5th SYMPHONY
SHUDDUP, GUYS, THEY'RE BACK!
HELLO DOGS!
WOOF! WOOF! WOOF!
YAP, YAP! YAP, YAP! YAP, YAP!
WOOF, WOOF, WOOF, WOOF, WOOF!
RF

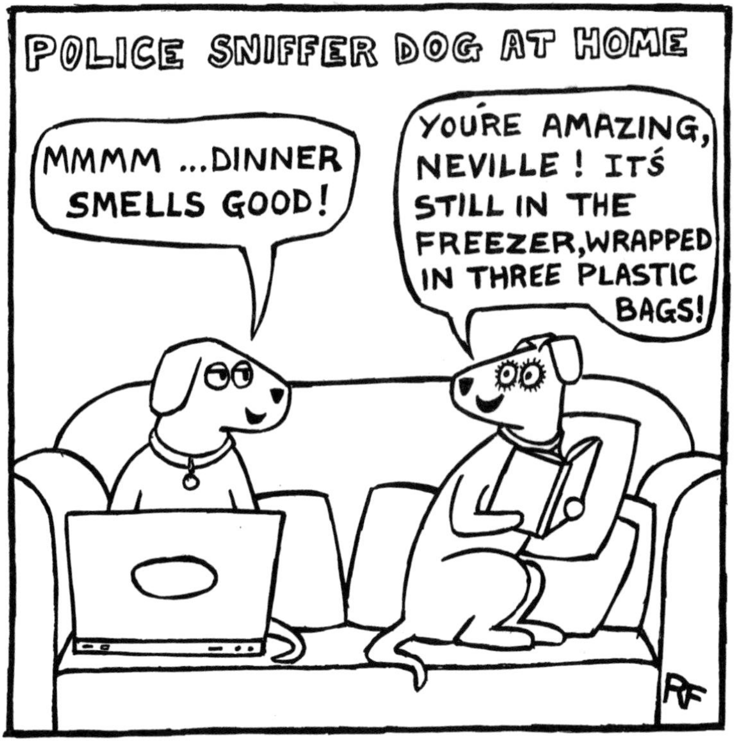
POLICE SNIFFER DOG AT HOME
MMMM ...DINNER SMELLS GOOD!
YOU'RE AMAZING, NEVILLE! IT'S STILL IN THE FREEZER, WRAPPED IN THREE PLASTIC BAGS!
RF

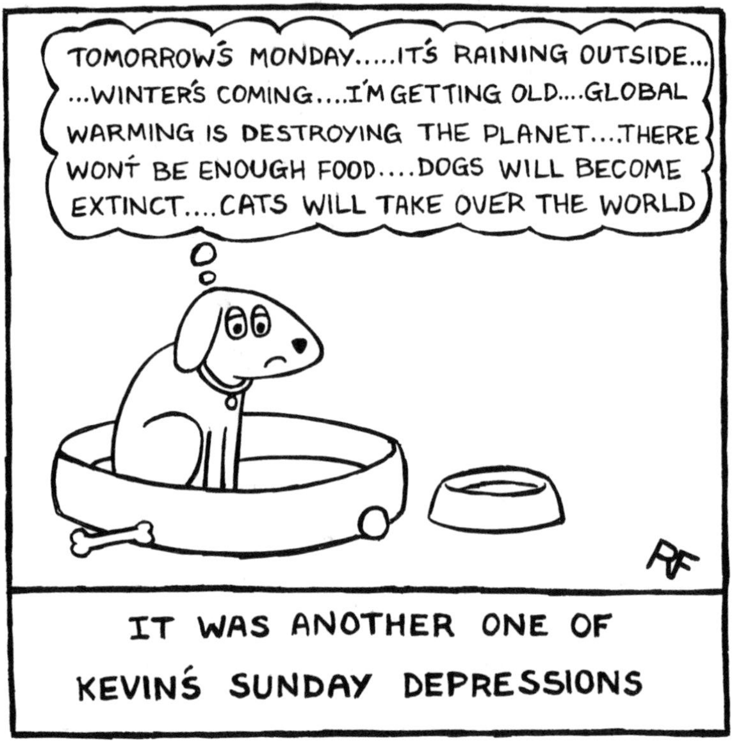
TOMORROW'S MONDAY.....IT'S RAINING OUTSIDE... ...WINTER'S COMING....I'M GETTING OLD....GLOBAL WARMING IS DESTROYING THE PLANET....THERE WON'T BE ENOUGH FOOD....DOGS WILL BECOME EXTINCT....CATS WILL TAKE OVER THE WORLD

IT WAS ANOTHER ONE OF KEVIN'S SUNDAY DEPRESSIONS

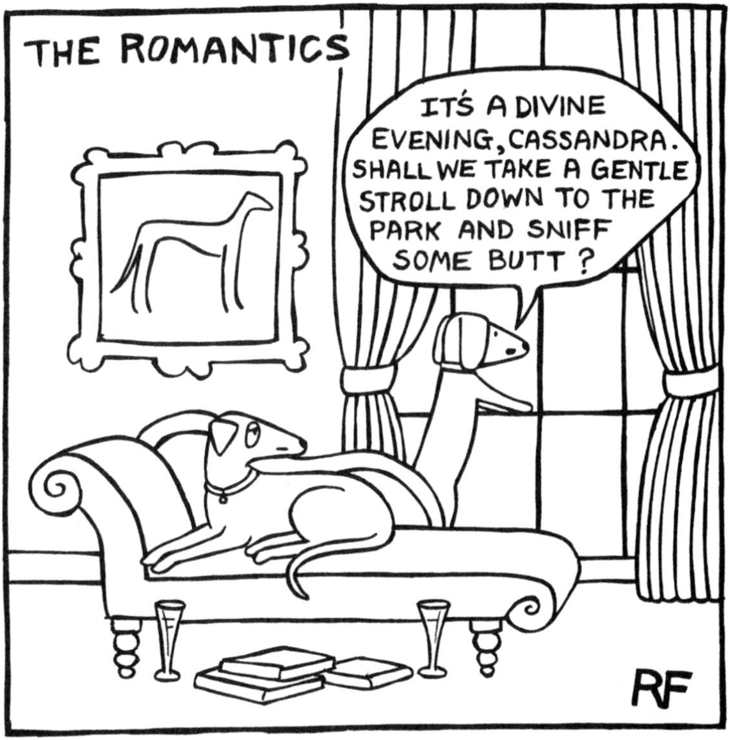
THE ROMANTICS
IT'S A DIVINE EVENING, CASSANDRA. SHALL WE TAKE A GENTLE STROLL DOWN TO THE PARK AND SNIFF SOME BUTT ?
RF

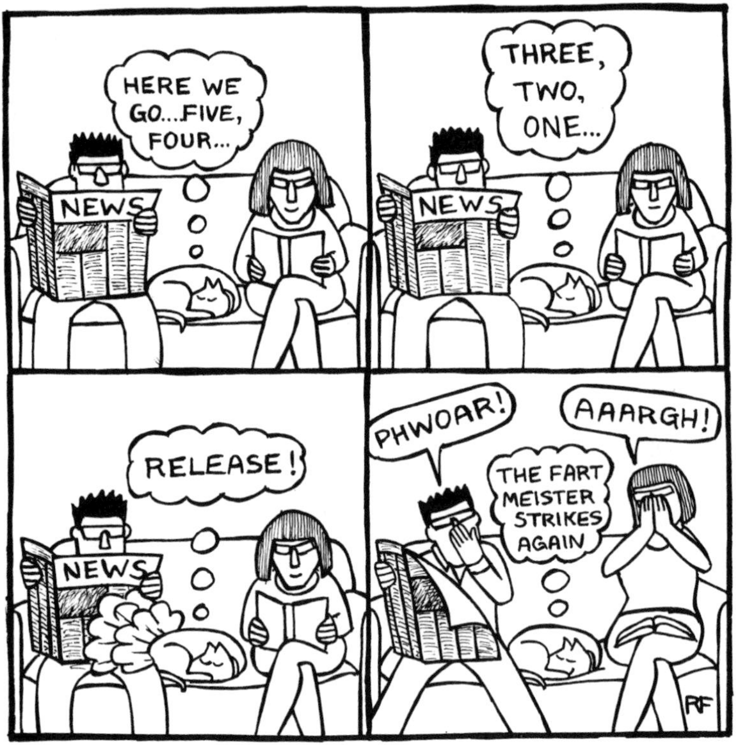
HERE WE GO... FIVE, FOUR...
NEWS
THREE, TWO, ONE...
NEWS
RELEASE!
NEWS
PHWOAR!
AAARGH!
THE FART MEISTER STRIKES AGAIN
RF

...THEN THIS BIG OBEDIENCE INSTRUCTOR WALKS OVER TO ME AND SHOUTS SIT!....SO I LOOKED UP AT HIM AND I SAID YOU SIT!...

THE HARD MEN OF 'D' WING SWAP WAR STORIES

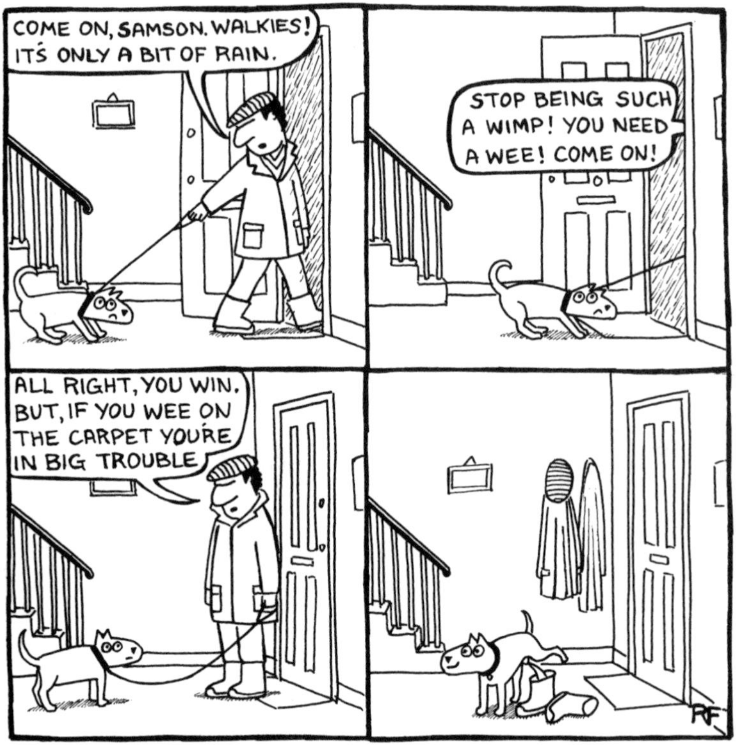
COME ON, SAMSON. WALKIES! ITS ONLY A BIT OF RAIN.
STOP BEING SUCH A WIMP! YOU NEED A WEE! COME ON!
ALL RIGHT, YOU WIN. BUT, IF YOU WEE ON THE CARPET YOU'RE IN BIG TROUBLE
RF

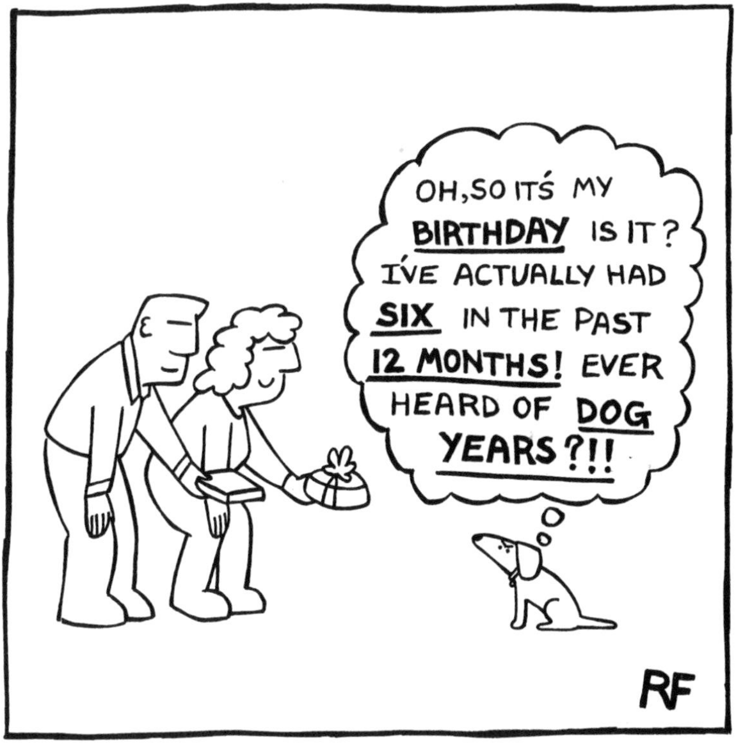
OH, SO IT'S MY BIRTHDAY IS IT? I'VE ACTUALLY HAD SIX IN THE PAST 12 MONTHS! EVER HEARD OF DOG YEARS?!!
RF

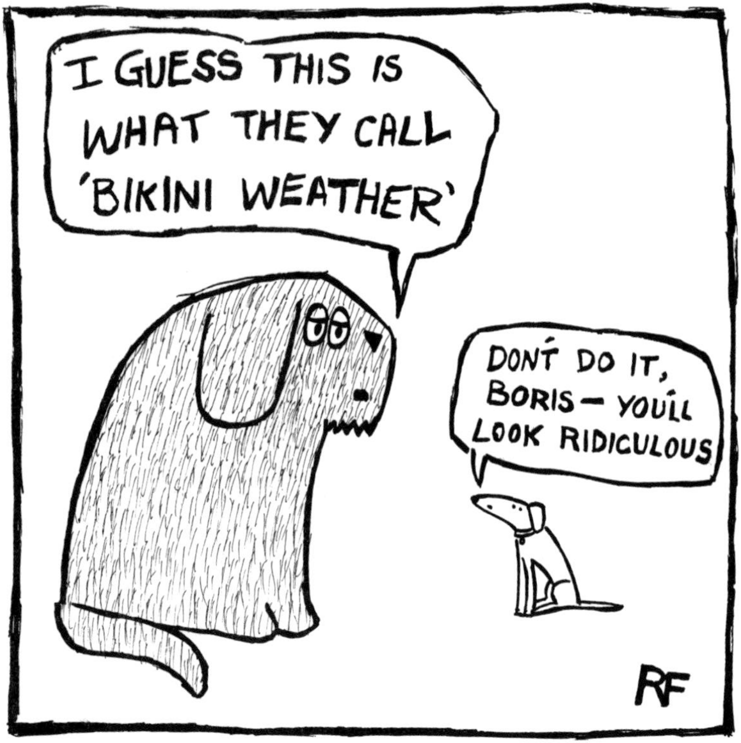
I GUESS THIS IS WHAT THEY CALL 'BIKINI WEATHER'
DON'T DO IT, BORIS— YOU'LL LOOK RIDICULOUS
RF

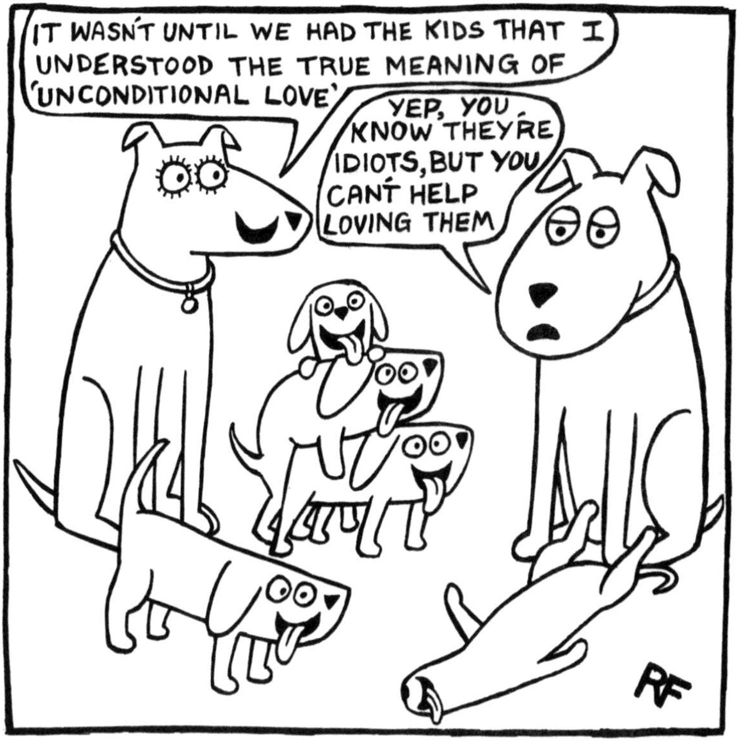
IT WASN'T UNTIL WE HAD THE KIDS THAT I UNDERSTOOD THE TRUE MEANING OF 'UNCONDITIONAL LOVE'
YEP, YOU KNOW THEY'RE IDIOTS, BUT YOU CAN'T HELP LOVING THEM
RF

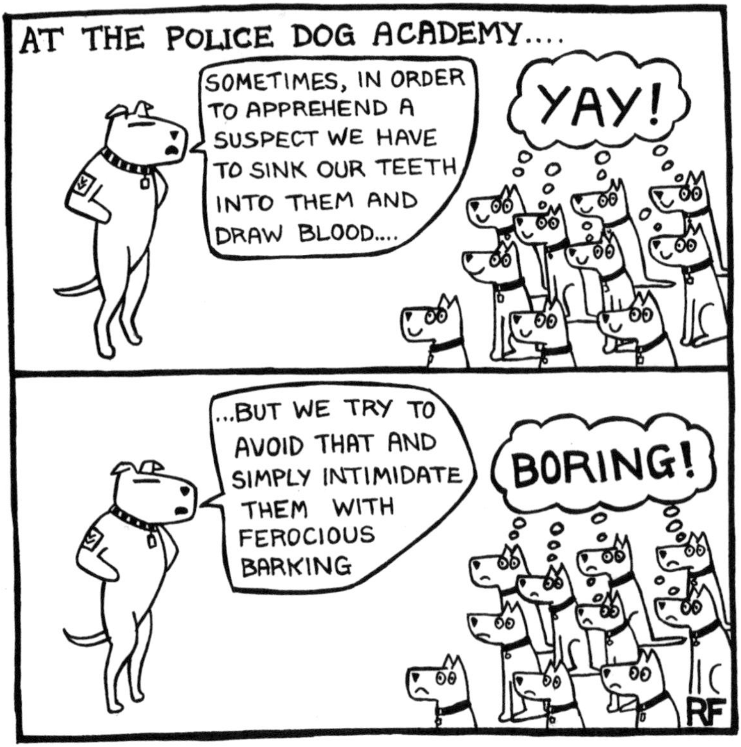
AT THE POLICE DOG ACADEMY....
SOMETIMES, IN ORDER TO APPREHEND A SUSPECT WE HAVE TO SINK OUR TEETH INTO THEM AND DRAW BLOOD....
YAY!
...BUT WE TRY TO AVOID THAT AND SIMPLY INTIMIDATE THEM WITH FEROCIOUS BARKING
BORING!
RF

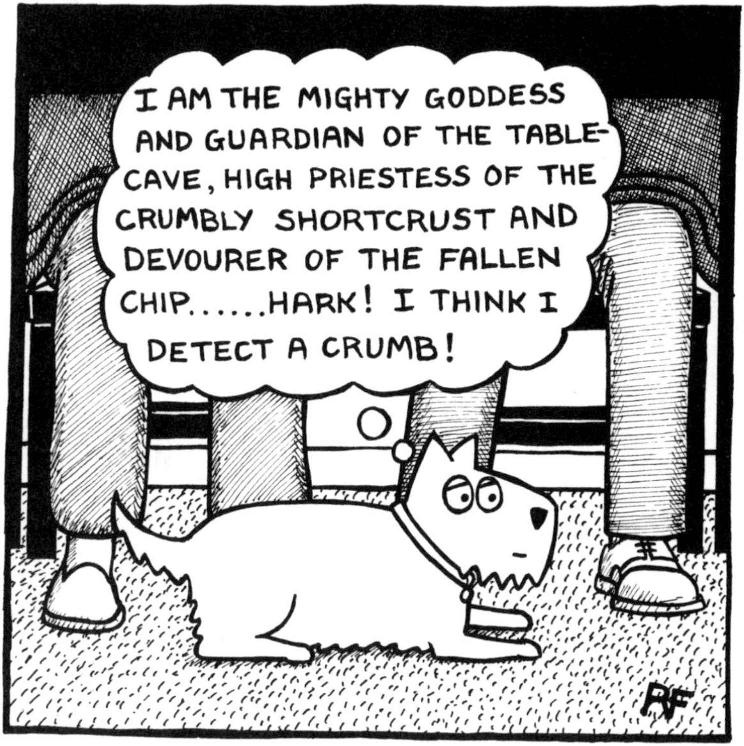
I AM THE MIGHTY GODDESS AND GUARDIAN OF THE TABLE-CAVE, HIGH PRIESTESS OF THE CRUMBLY SHORTCRUST AND DEVOURER OF THE FALLEN CHIP......HARK! I THINK I DETECT A CRUMB!
RF

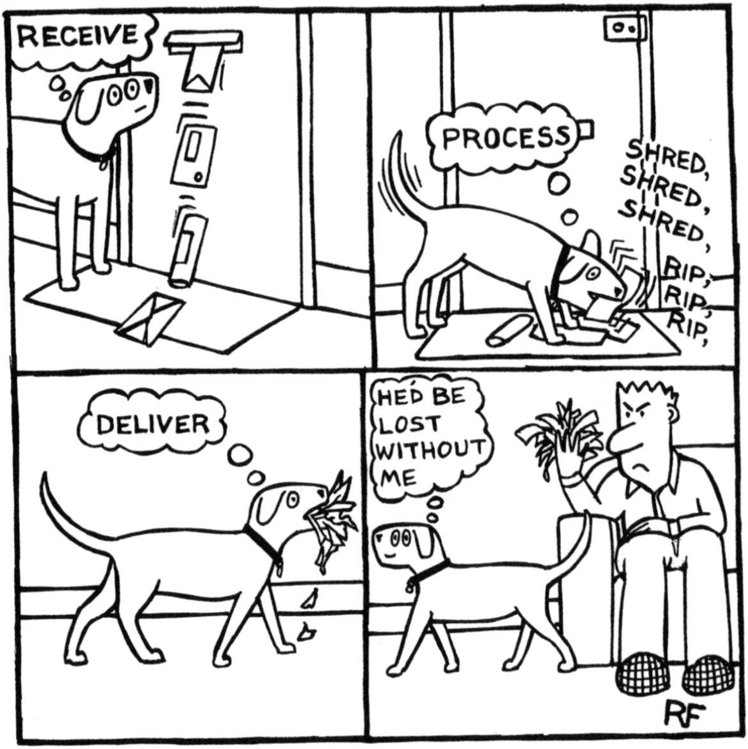
RECEIVE
PROCESS
SHRED, SHRED, SHRED,
RIP, RIP, RIP,
DELIVER
HE'D BE LOST WITHOUT ME
RF

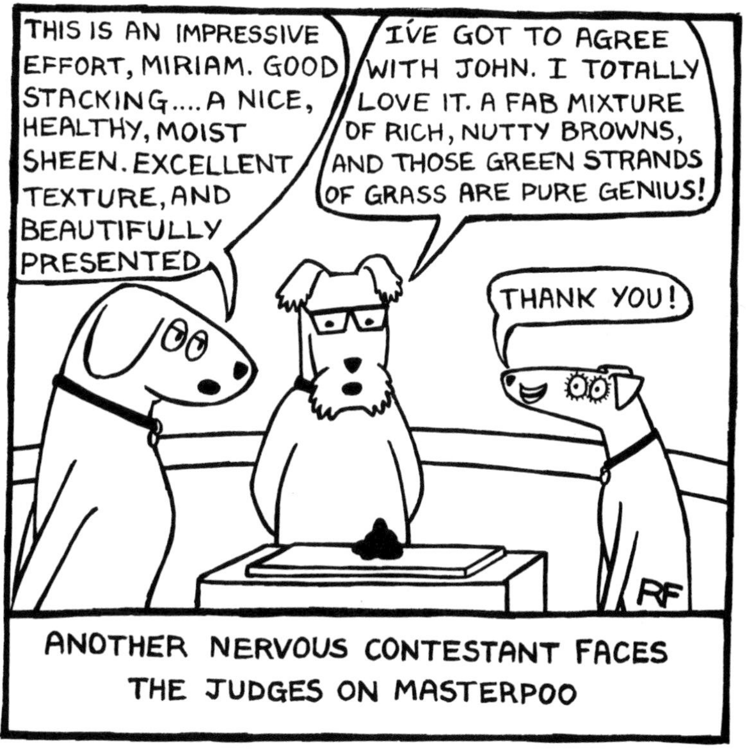
THIS IS AN IMPRESSIVE EFFORT, MIRIAM. GOOD STACKING.... A NICE, HEALTHY, MOIST SHEEN. EXCELLENT TEXTURE, AND BEAUTIFULLY PRESENTED
I'VE GOT TO AGREE WITH JOHN. I TOTALLY LOVE IT. A FAB MIXTURE OF RICH, NUTTY BROWNS, AND THOSE GREEN STRANDS OF GRASS ARE PURE GENIUS!
THANK YOU!
RF

ANOTHER NERVOUS CONTESTANT FACES THE JUDGES ON MASTERPOO

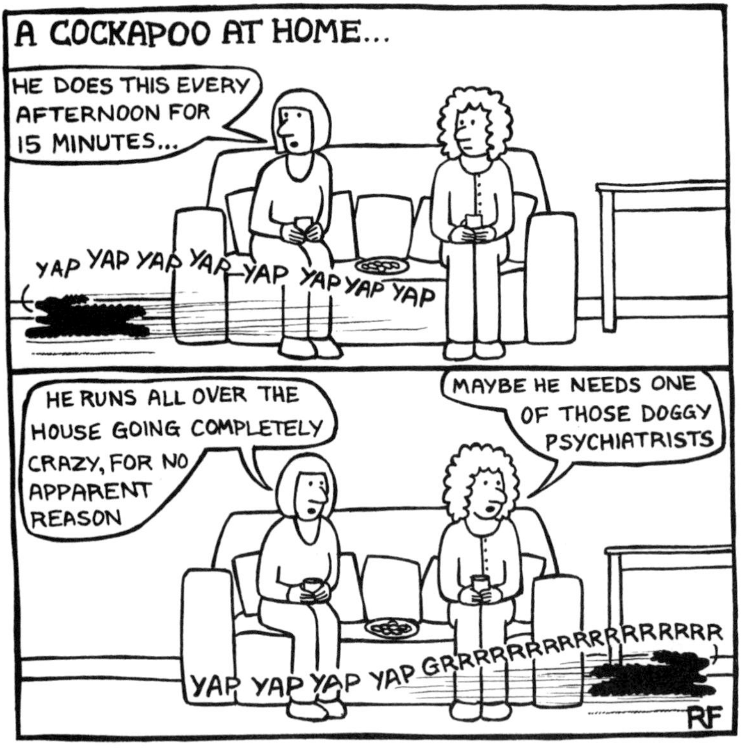
A COCKAPOO AT HOME...
HE DOES THIS EVERY AFTERNOON FOR 15 MINUTES...
YAP YAP YAP YAP YAP YAP YAP YAP YAP
HE RUNS ALL OVER THE HOUSE GOING COMPLETELY CRAZY, FOR NO APPARENT REASON
MAYBE HE NEEDS ONE OF THOSE DOGGY PSYCHIATRISTS
YAP YAP YAP YAP GRRRRRRRRRRRRRRRRRRR
RF

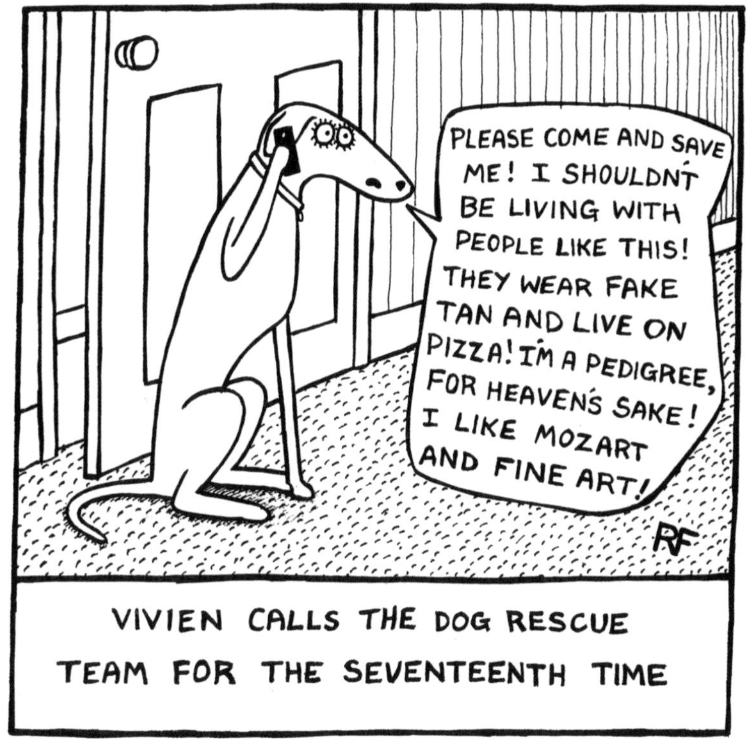
PLEASE COME AND SAVE ME! I SHOULDN'T BE LIVING WITH PEOPLE LIKE THIS! THEY WEAR FAKE TAN AND LIVE ON PIZZA! I'M A PEDIGREE, FOR HEAVEN'S SAKE! I LIKE MOZART AND FINE ART!
RF

VIVIEN CALLS THE DOG RESCUE TEAM FOR THE SEVENTEENTH TIME

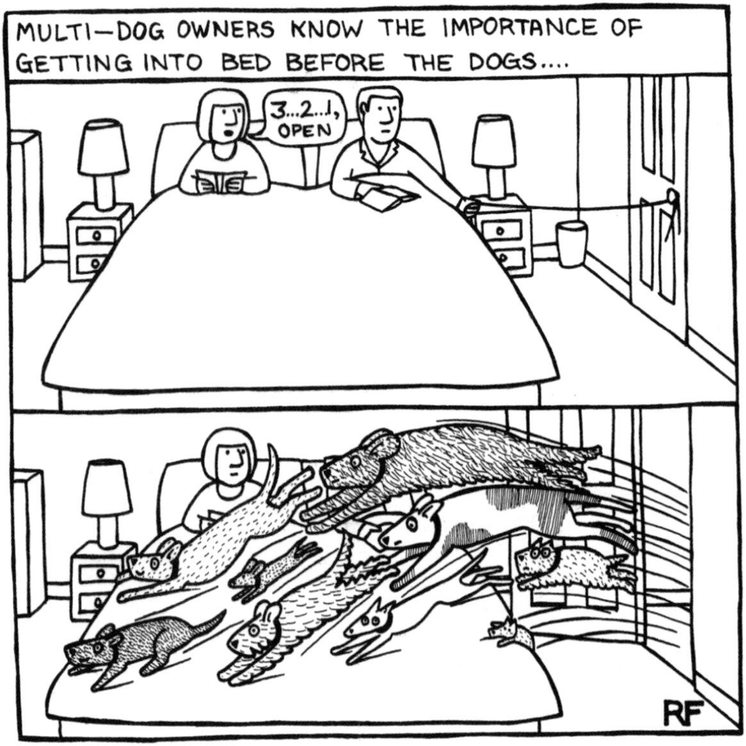
MULTI—DOG OWNERS KNOW THE IMPORTANCE OF GETTING INTO BED BEFORE THE DOGS....
3...2...1, OPEN
RF

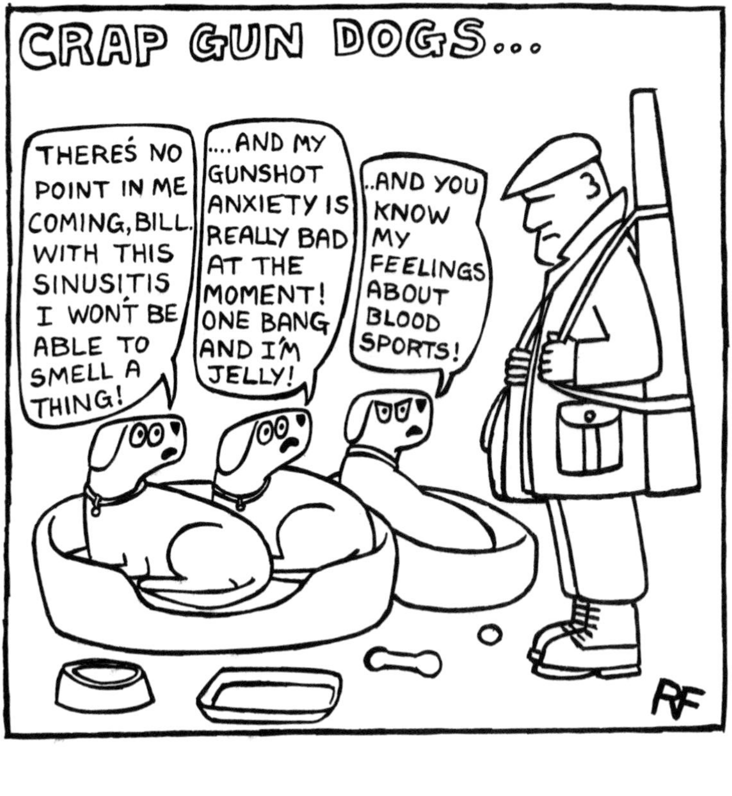
CRAP GUN DOGS...
THERE'S NO POINT IN ME COMING, BILL. WITH THIS SINUSITIS I WON'T BE ABLE TO SMELL A THING!
....AND MY GUNSHOT ANXIETY IS REALLY BAD AT THE MOMENT! ONE BANG AND I'M JELLY!
..AND YOU KNOW MY FEELINGS ABOUT BLOOD SPORTS!
RF

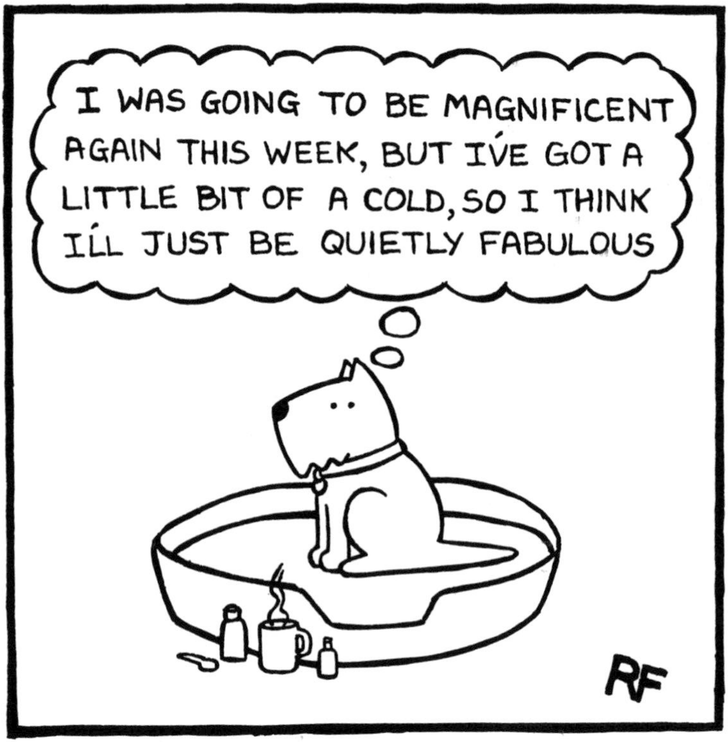
I WAS GOING TO BE MAGNIFICENT AGAIN THIS WEEK, BUT I'VE GOT A LITTLE BIT OF A COLD, SO I THINK I'LL JUST BE QUIETLY FABULOUS
RF

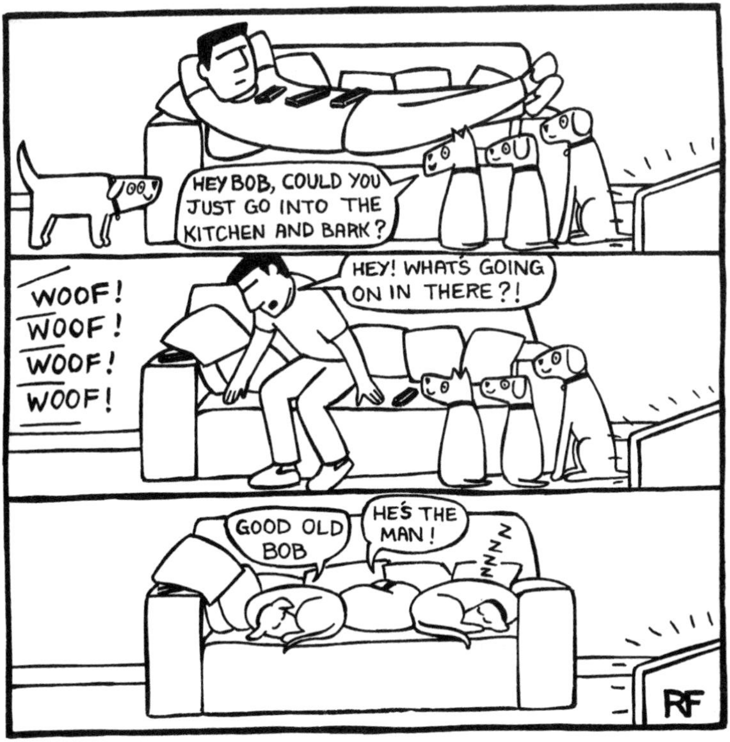
HEY BOB, COULD YOU JUST GO INTO THE KITCHEN AND BARK?
WOOF! WOOF! WOOF! WOOF!
HEY! WHAT'S GOING ON IN THERE?!
GOOD OLD BOB
HE'S THE MAN!
ZZZZ
RF

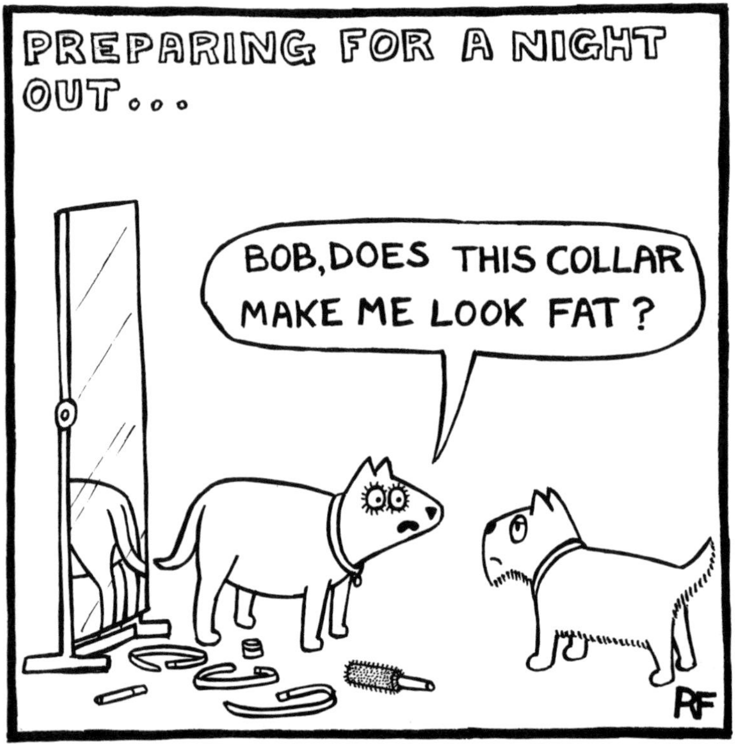
PREPARING FOR A NIGHT OUT...
BOB, DOES THIS COLLAR MAKE ME LOOK FAT?
RF

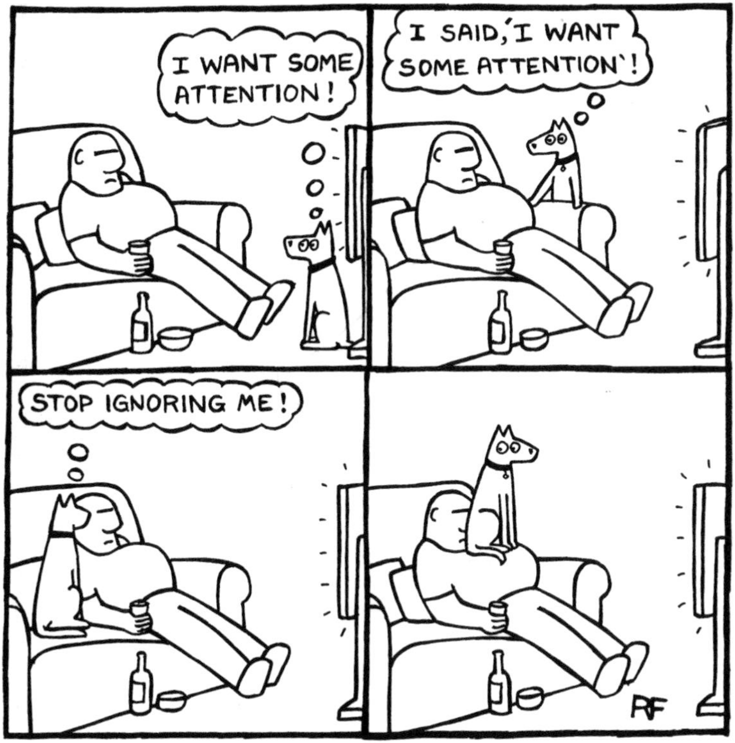
I WANT SOME ATTENTION!
I SAID, 'I WANT SOME ATTENTION'!
STOP IGNORING ME!
RF

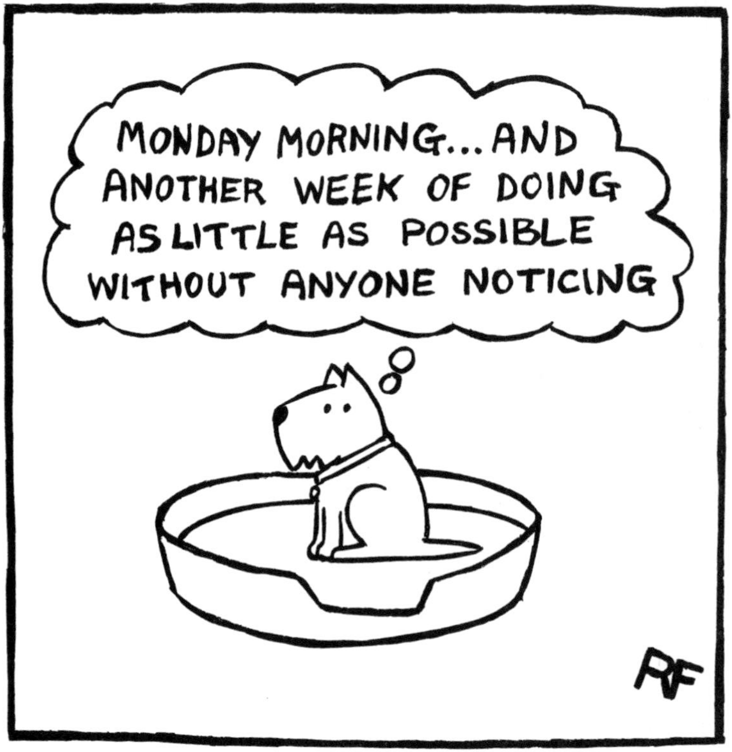
MONDAY MORNING... AND ANOTHER WEEK OF DOING AS LITTLE AS POSSIBLE WITHOUT ANYONE NOTICING
RF

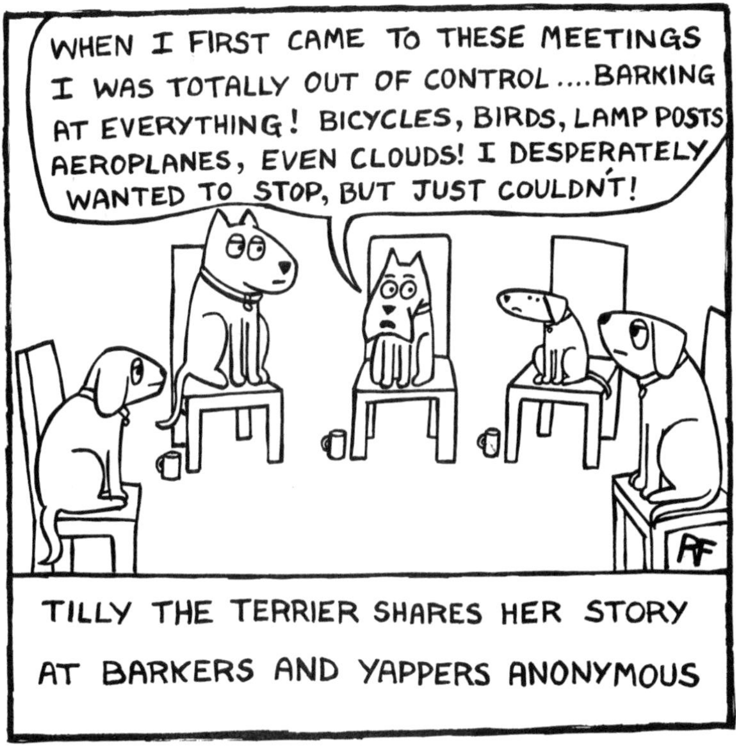
WHEN I FIRST CAME TO THESE MEETINGS I WAS TOTALLY OUT OF CONTROL ....BARKING AT EVERYTHING! BICYCLES, BIRDS, LAMP POSTS AEROPLANES, EVEN CLOUDS! I DESPERATELY WANTED TO STOP, BUT JUST COULDN'T!
RF

TILLY THE TERRIER SHARES HER STORY AT BARKERS AND YAPPERS ANONYMOUS

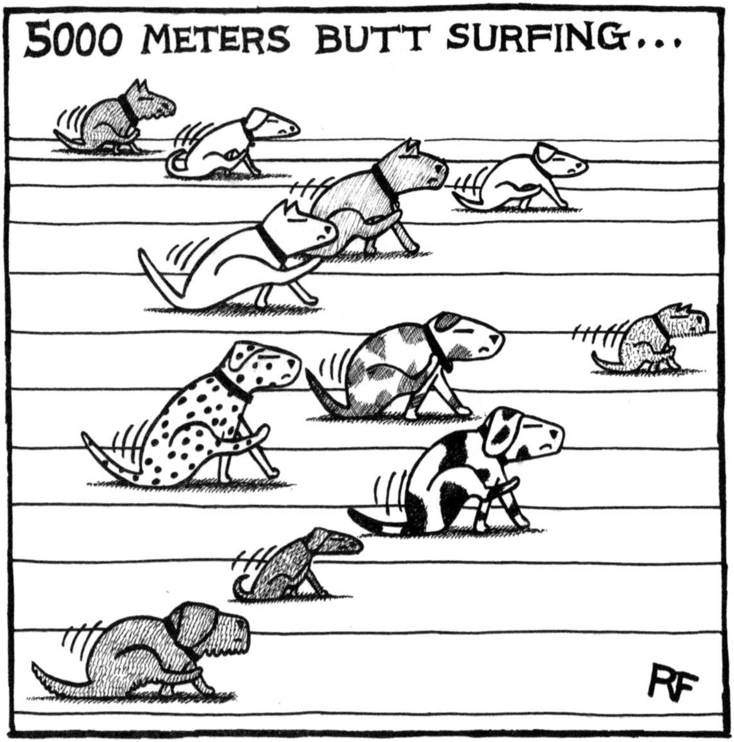
5000 METERS BUTT SURFING...
RF

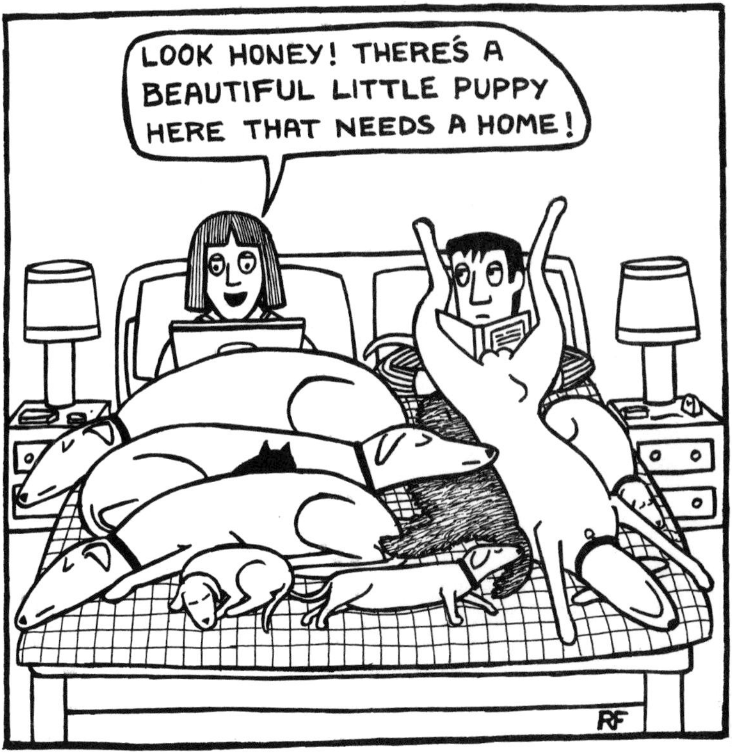
LOOK HONEY! THERE'S A BEAUTIFUL LITTLE PUPPY HERE THAT NEEDS A HOME!
RF

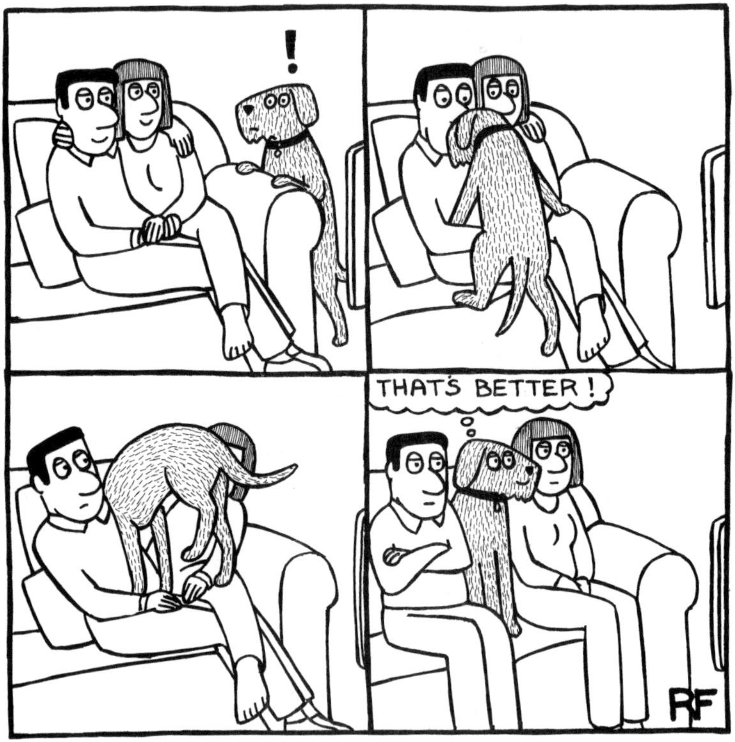
!
THAT'S BETTER!
RF

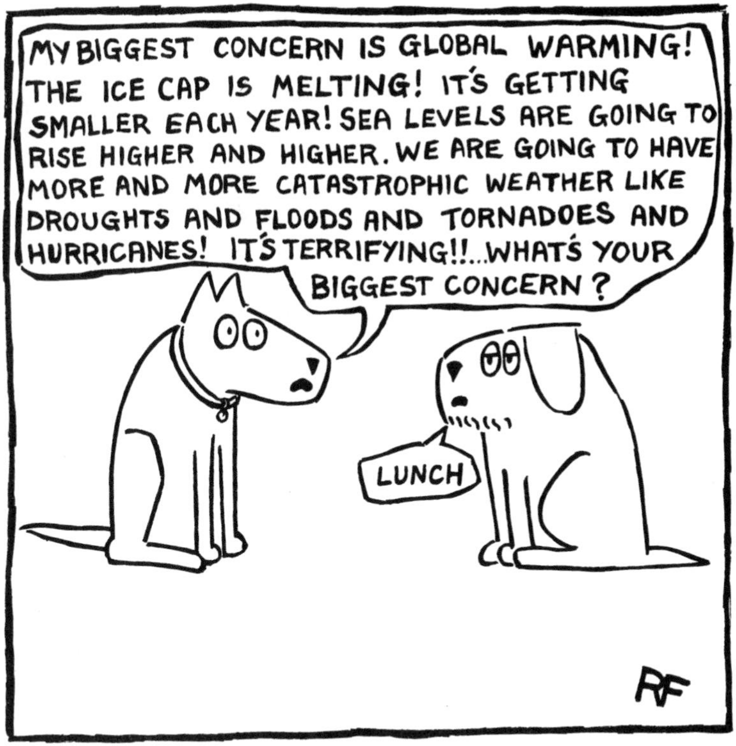
MY BIGGEST CONCERN IS GLOBAL WARMING! THE ICE CAP IS MELTING! IT'S GETTING SMALLER EACH YEAR! SEA LEVELS ARE GOING TO RISE HIGHER AND HIGHER. WE ARE GOING TO HAVE MORE AND MORE CATASTROPHIC WEATHER LIKE DROUGHTS AND FLOODS AND TORNADOES AND HURRICANES! IT'S TERRIFYING!!...WHAT'S YOUR BIGGEST CONCERN?
LUNCH
RF

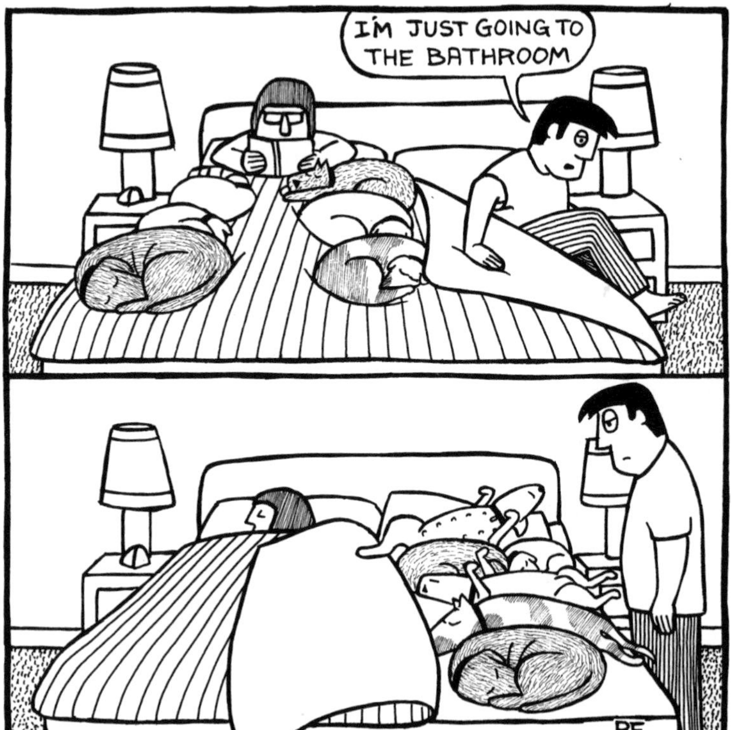
I'M JUST GOING TO THE BATHROOM
RF

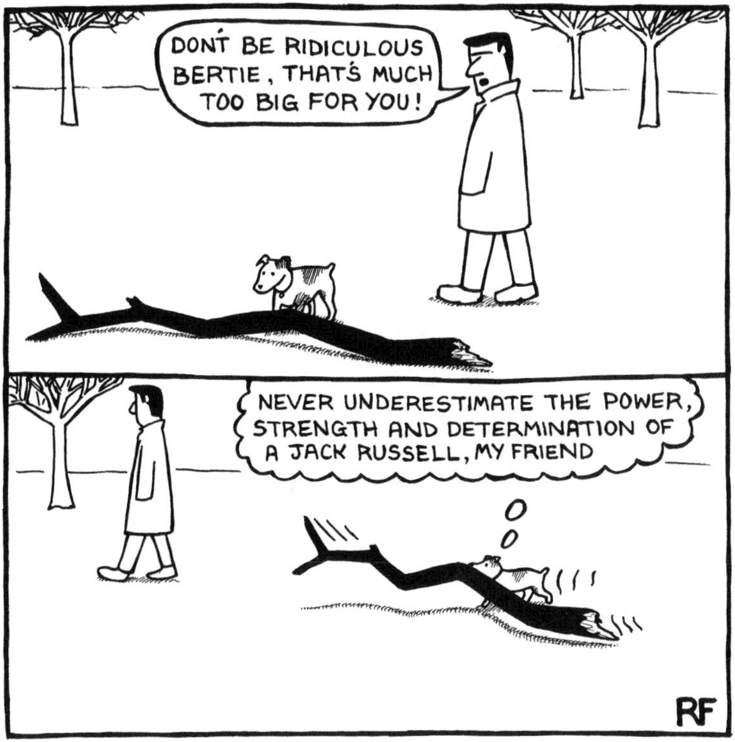
DON'T BE RIDICULOUS BERTIE, THAT'S MUCH TOO BIG FOR YOU!
NEVER UNDERESTIMATE THE POWER, STRENGTH AND DETERMINATION OF A JACK RUSSELL, MY FRIEND
RF

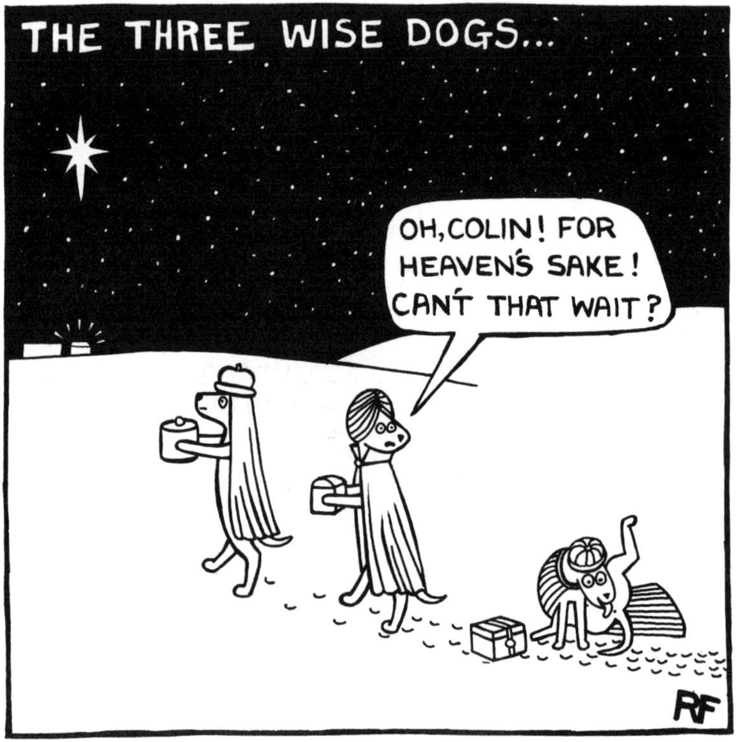
THE THREE WISE DOGS...
OH, COLIN! FOR HEAVEN'S SAKE! CAN'T THAT WAIT?
RF

About the author

Rupert Fawcett became a professional cartoonist almost by accident when in 1989, whilst doodling, he drew a bald man in braces and carpet slippers and called him Fred. The Fred cartoons went on to be syndicated in the *Mail on Sunday* and published in several books. To date more than 9 million Fred greetings cards have been sold in the UK, Australia and New Zealand. Off The Leash is his latest creation.

www.rupertfawcettcartoons.com
www.facebook.com/OffTheLeashDailyDogCartoons